HUMAN RIGHTS IN
THE UNITED KINGDOM

Human Rights in the United Kingdom

RICHARD GORDON QC

and

RICHARD WILMOT-SMITH QC

OXFORD UNIVERSITY PRESS
1996

Oxford University Press, Great Clarendon Street, Oxford OX2 6DP

Oxford New York

Athens Auckland Bangkok Bogota Bombay
Buenos Aires Calcutta Cape Town Dar es Salaam
Delhi Florence Hong Kong Istanbul Karachi
Kuala Lumpur Madras Madrid Melbourne
Mexico City Nairobi Paris Singapore
Taipei Tokyo Toronto
and associated companies in
Berlin Ibadan

Oxford is a trade mark of Oxford University Press

Published in the United States by
Oxford University Press Inc., New York

British Library Cataloguing in Publication Data
Data available

Library of Congress Cataloging in Publication Data
Data available

ISBN 0-19-826067-9

1 3 5 7 9 10 8 6 4 2

Typeset by Best-set Typesetter Ltd., Hong Kong
Printed in Great Britain by
Bookcraft Ltd., Midsomer Norton, Avon.

Contents

Foreword

Writing in September 1996 with a general election approaching, it appears probable that the political debate will focus increasingly on three issues, each of which could have important constitutional implications for this country. The issues are not exactly new but they could produce fundamental changes in our political and legal system.

The issues concern; this country's relationship with the European Union, devolution in Wales and Scotland; and the incorporation of a domestic bill of human rights. They have the common feature that, at present at any rate, they are among the limited number of topics where there is a significant difference of approach between the government and the opposition parties. It appears likely that the two principal opposition parties will enter the election committed to closer integration with Europe and to constitutional reform involving devolution and the incorporation of a bill of rights, but these will be opposed by the party which is at present in power.

This book is primarily concerned with the human rights issue. However if the opposition parties' policy on the other two issues becomes the policy of the government then the case of the incorporation of a bill of rights will, in my view, be considerably strengthened. There are a number of reasons for this. First of all some of the arguments against the incorporation of a bill of rights are based on the extent to which this would interfere with the sovereignty of Parliament. On the other side arguments can be advanced for saying that for Parliament to surrender certain areas of its supremacy as a legislator far from being inconsistent with, in fact confirms its sovereignty. Whether you accept .this view or not, Parliament's supremacy is already affected by our membership of the European Union and this effect will be increased if this country is a party to the greater integration within the Union which is now proposed. Further integration will also accelerate the process of introducing the European Convention of Human Rights into our domestic law as part of European Community law.[1] In addition the devolution which is proposed will involve an express surrender of sovereignty. While in theory what Parliament can achieve by legislating on

---

[1] See Lord Bingham's Contribution at p. 10 where he refers to Lord Slynn of Hadley's speech in the House of Lords.

devolution could be undone by further legislation in practice this is a remote possibility.

Both closer integration with the other members of the European Union and devolution will also undermine another argument advanced by those opposed to incorporation of a bill of rights. This is that it will change the role of the judiciary, because the judiciary will inevitably by required to adjudicate as to whether Parliament has trespassed into areas where it has surrendered its powers either to Europe or Scotland and Wales. It is therefore not surprising that the political parties which are in favour of closer involvement in Europe and devolution also favour a United Kingdom bill of rights. However even if you are in favour in principle of the incorporation of a bill of rights there still remain important questions to be answered. What form should the incorporation take? Do we follow the precedent of our joining the Common Market and merely adopt the European Convention as it stands? Or should we devise our own convention basing it on the European Convention but recognising that that convention is now being increasingly recognised as having shortcomings? Should there be different or additional rights which are protected? It is also necessary to decide the extent of the protection which will be provided by the bill. Should we follow the New Zealand example which only provides protection where existing or future legislation is capable of being interpreted in a manner which is consistent with the Bill? Should we follow the example provided by the Canadian Charter which allows legislation to override Charter rights where this is expressly stated to be the intention, even if in practice this rarely happens. What about the courts which are to adjudicate on the rights? Should any court from Richmond Magistrates Court to the House of Lords be able to override legislation passed by Parliament or should this power, for example, be limited to a new constitutional court which consists of judges with different qualifications who are selected by a new and different process? What remedies should be provided in the case of a breach? Should they be those at present available on an application for judicial review or should they be more extensive, including for example compensation as is the case with the European Court of Human Rights?

Unfortunately many lawyers (including judges) and parliamentarians and a great majority of the public have not considered these questions and are largely ignorant as to what are the implications of incorporating a Bill of Rights. If they share my good fortune in being able to read the contributions contained in this book, they will be much better informed and will find this a most stimulating and informative experience. The contributors all support incorporation but they approach the subject from different vantage points, relying on their particular expertise, whether acquired as a judge, a lawyer, an academic or a political commentator. Collectively they cover the majority of the arguments and provide the information which is needed for an informed debate, the need for which is overwhelming. It would be regrettable indeed if decisions were reached on these issues without the full implications being properly considered since once the decisions have been taken, they are almost inevitably going to be irreversible. The incorporation of the Bills of Rights should not be open to the same criticism as is frequently heard as to our membership of the European Community, that "I never realised what was involved".

The subject is too important for that. After all it could result in Professor Dworkin being proved to be correct when he states as part of his distinguished contribution that:

Incorporation would put the special skills of British lawyers and judges, and the heritage of British legal principle at the service of the civilised world. Britain could become once again a leader in defining and protecting individual freedom. Instead of, as a sullen defendant, giving ground to liberty only when ordered to do so by a foreign Court.

The Rt. Hon. the Lord Woolf,
The Master of the Rolls
Royal Courts of Justice
September, 1996

Introduction

We want to present, in accessible form and to as wide a public as possible, the important arguments in favour of the incorporation of the European Convention on Human Rights into our law. With a General Election close, we want there to be an informative but non-technical book which clearly and interestingly looks at the arguments concerning incorporation and does so in a manner suitable for the general but well informed reader. There is not easily available, and in one place, a statement of what those in favour of incorporation are actually saying and how they deal with the various arguments opposed to them. Furthermore a copy of the Convention itself is not easily found save within specialist titles on sale in legal book-shops, and even those are not easy to locate. This is remarkable. There is great interest in the issue. Two out of the three main parties support incorporation and recent opinion polls show that about 80% of the public support it. A collection of essays which deals with these matters fills a real gap in the available literature on the subject of human rights generally.

Incorporation is not an academic or a lawyer's issue. It goes to the heart of the relationship of citizens to the Government and, increasingly, to the relationship between citizens themselves.

We thought that the question of incorporation should be approached from different perspectives, and not only from lawyers. The contributions from Andrew Marr, Editor of *The Independent*, and Bill Emmott and David Manasian, Editor and writer respectively for *The Economist*, give the debate the added dimension that such important figures in the field of political journalism can give.

Andrew Marr's essay considers whether we need more than ratification but additionally a Bill of Rights of our own, looks back in time at the origins of rights-based politics and then ahead at the future of the "rights agenda" in Britain. He sets out three criteria for the creation of new rights: consensus, affordability and clarity and closes with the suggestion that duties of citizens could be usefully appended to a new Bill of Rights. The question of there being imposed upon citizens duties as well as their enjoying rights is explored in other essays.

The essay by Bill Emmott and David Manasian looks at the topic from both a historical and journalistic perspective. They look at and compare the nineteenth century view of the constitution put forward by Dicey with the current position of Parliament where power is concentrated in the executive. They conclude with the interesting but persuasive view that, contrary to the current political situation, a Bill of Rights should be more prized by the parties of right than those of the left.

Given the fact that nearly fifty years have passed since the Convention was drafted and ratified, it is inevitable that consideration should also be given to whether the Convention is a sufficient statement of what ought to be the rights of citizens. Therefore two contributions consider whether there should be a domestic Bill of Rights which confers rights beyond those to be found in the Convention.

John Wadham sets out a number of rights missing from the Convention which he says ought to be included within a British Bill of Rights (the right to information and the right of a fair trial in the extradition system before deportation, for example) and goes on to consider the need for us to create our own mechanisms to draft and implement our own domestic Bill of Rights. Francesca Klug's essay considers this question from the perspective of whether there should be duties upon citizens as well as rights, expanding upon one of Andrew Marr's themes. In her view incorporation would not simply create rights but would also create duties of citizens. The rights set out in the convention are not to be looked at in a vacuum, she says, but are to be balanced with the rights and duties of other individuals and the needs of society as a whole. In the course of her essay she looks effectively at the views of Professor Etzioni who, in the United States, has called for a moratorium on the "minting" of new rights.

Lord Bingham, the newly appointed Lord Chief Justice, presents, in the reprint of his Denning Lecture, the arguments for incorporation. In an approach mirrored by other contributors he looks also at the arguments against incorporation and holds them up to the light of his inexorable logic. His outstanding essay cannot be read without noting that his predecessor as Lord Chief Justice and his successor as Master of the Rolls are both also enthusiastic proponents of incorporation.

Professor Ronald Dworkin in his powerful and important essay asks and answers the question "Does Britain Need a Bill of Rights". He then considers that the simplest way in which a genuine British Bill of Rights can be created is by the expedient of incorporating the Convention into our law and examines the constitutional position and the arguments against incorporation. His essay is as elegant and compelling as one would expect from such a great but popular academic. It is interesting to compare Professor Dworkin's analysis of the arguments against incorporation with those of Lord Bingham. Professor Dworkin is looking at the issue from the point of view of an United States citizen. In the United States the Bill of Rights is part of the constitution and is therefore the birthright of all citizens. This gives force to his view that the most important benefit of incorporation would be "a revitalization of the liberty and dignity of the people . . ."

Our own contributions take different perspectives. Richard Gordon Q.C. looks at the constitutional position, where, he says, that modern judicial review lacks a constitutional dimension for the protection of human rights and then explains why, in his view, we need a constitutional court. It is remarkable that this country does not have a constitutional court, which is thought to be an essential part of the fabric of so many democracies. Richard Wilmot-Smith Q.C. looks at the absence of incorporation as a national conceit best discarded and examines some of the arguments put up against incorporation in the 1978 Report of the Select Committee of the House of Lords on a Bill of Rights.

Appropriately, the collection is concluded by Lord Lester Q.C., who for many years has championed the cause of incorporation and is now able to do so in the House of Lords. He provides, in a reprint of his Paul Sieghart Lecture, a thoroughly researched commentary on the attitude of important members of the 1950 the Labour Government to the Convention. One said that the Convention had to be woven into the fabric of our law and another, shortly thereafter, said that legislation was not necessary to give effect to the terms of the Convention. The latter view prevailed. This is why forty six years later, there is the need for this book. A theme of several other essays, namely the vigilance of citizens in holding ministers and officials to account, is taken up by Lord Lester who recommends a parliamentary Select Committee on Human Rights as well as incorporating the Convention.

We have already noted that Lord Bingham's successor as Master of the Rolls is also a strong proponent of incorporation. We are grateful to him for agreeing to write the Foreword. Lord Bingham's immediate predecessor as Lord Chief Justice, Lord Taylor of Gosforth, also an advocate for incorporation, originally agreed to write the Foreword. We regret that illness has prevented him from doing so. We wish him well and dedicate this book to him.

10th September 1996

Richard Gordon Q.C.
Richard Wilmot-Smith Q.C.

39 Essex Street,
London WC2A 3AT.

1

The European Convention on Human Rights: Time To Incorporate[1]

THE RIGHT HON. LORD BINGHAM, LORD CHIEF JUSTICE

I would confidently hope that human rights, the subject of this lecture, qualifies as a suitable subject for a Denning Lecture, and I am reassured to know that the argument I shall be advancing is one which Lord Denning, after some initial hesitation, came to support.[2] For there is no task more central to the purpose of a modern democracy, or more central to the judicial function, than that of seeking to protect, within the law, the basic human rights of the citizen, against invasion by other citizens or by the state itself. I hope this point is too obvious to need labouring. But I cannot resist two quotations. The first is from an Italian lawyer, who wrote (perhaps significantly) during the 1930s that

The state finds its highest expression in protecting rights, and therefore should be grateful to the citizen who, in demanding justice, gives it the opportunity to defend justice, which after all is the basic *raison d'être* of the State.[3]

The second quotation is from the agreed statement issued at the end of an international conference on human rights, over which the Lord Chancellor presided, held in Oxford in September 1992:

In democratic societies fundamental human rights and freedoms are more than paper aspirations. They form part of the law. And it is the special province of judges to see to it that the law's undertakings are realised in the daily life of the people.[4]

When, as sometimes happens, one right conflicts with another (the right of free expression, for instance, with the right to privacy) then the judge has, so far as the law allows, to reconcile the two.

---

[1] This essay reproduces Lord Bingham's Denning Lecture given at the Middle Temple Hall on 2 March 1993.

[2] Anthony Lester, QC, 'Fundamental Rights: The United Kingdom Isolated?' [1984] P.L. 63, 83.

[3] Piero Calamandrei, *Eulogy of Judges* (Princeton University Press, 1942).

[4] *Balliol Statement of 1992* (23 September 1992), para. 6.

Human Rights and the Constitution

I would suggest that the ability of English judges to protect human rights in this country and reconcile conflicting rights in the manner indicated is inhibited by the failure of successive governments over many years to incorporate into United Kingdom law the European Convention on Human Rights and Fundamental Freedoms. But I should like, in the manner of the modern fast bowler, to take a rather lengthy run up to that question, making some preliminary observations about the constitution.

Lord Hailsham, I think, once observed that judges are usually illiterate in constitutional matters. I shall therefore preface my observations with a health warning. But I shall not talk a great deal of rubbish on this particular subject because I shall not say a great deal about it at all.

Most of us, I suspect, were reared on a fairly straightforward Diceyan concept of the constitution. The centrepiece of this was of course a sovereign Parliament, able to do anything except make a man a woman or a woman a man. The executive was another arm of government, but not a separate arm since it was controlled by ministers who were of necessity members of one or other House of Parliament. The third horse of the troika was the judiciary, separate from legislature and executive save for the anomalous position of the Lord Chancellor and (in theory, not in practice) the Law Lords, and bound to interpret and apply the law of the land including of course the law made by Parliament. Over all, as the ultimate source of power and authority, was the Crown.

On this view the protection of human rights would have been seen as first and foremost the business of Parliament: if a government were to propose or permit any derogation from fundamental human rights, then it could expect to be restrained and even voted down in Parliament.

Much of this picture remains accurate. But constitutional organs, like constellations, wax and wane and change position relative to each other and the present century has seen such changes in our constitutional arrangements. Most striking has been the increase in the size and power of the executive, in particular the Prime Minister, the cabinet and ministers. Almost equally striking has been the weakening of parliamentary influence on the conduct of governments. For this there are no doubt many explanations, but the decline of the truly independent member, the doctrine of the electoral mandate, the tightening of party discipline, and the less deferential attitude of constituency parties are probably among them. At the same time Parliament, in practice is not in theory, has ceded a part of its sovereignty: for the first time ever a secular body beyond the mountains can bindingly declare Acts of Parliament to be unlawful. And the increase of executive power has been matched by a degree of judicial review unthinkable even a few years ago.

Where does all this leave the protection of human rights? Not in a very satisfactory position, I would suggest. The elective dictatorship of the majority means that, by and large, the government of the day can get its way, even if its majority is small. If its programme or its practice involves some derogation from human rights Parliament cannot be relied on to correct this. Nor can the judges. If the derogation springs from a statute, they must faithfully apply the statute. If it is a result of administrative practice, there may well be no basis upon which they can interfere. There is no higher law, no frame of reference, to which they can properly appeal. None of this matters very much if human rights themselves are not thought to matter very much. But if the protection of its citizens' fundamental rights is genuinely seen as an important function of civil society, then it does matter. In saying this I do not suggest—and I must stress this—that the present government or any of its predecessors has acted with wilful or cynical disregard of fundamental human rights. I would adopt and apply by analogy what Samuel Johnson said about truth: 'It is more from carelessness about truth than from intentional lying that there is so much falsehood in the world'. What I do suggest is that a government intent on implementing a programme may overlook the human rights aspects of its policies and that, if a government of more sinister intent were to gain power, we should be defenceless. There would not, certainly, be much the judges could do about it. This would seem regrettable to those who, like me, would see the judges as properly playing an important part in this field.

Two factors give the question a special immediacy. The first of these is the parliamentary timetable. The pressure on parliamentary time is such that measures to remedy violations of human rights will not, in the ordinary way, find a place in the queue. They will not have featured in the party manifesto. They will not win elections. They command no political priority. If anyone doubts this, I would refer to the thirty-eight reports of the Law Commission which awaited implementation in 1993. These reports, produced at quite considerable public expense, represent clear, well-argued and compelling proposals for improving the law; only two of the thirty-eight had been specifically rejected by the government of the day; they gather dust not because their value is doubted but because there is inadequate parliamentary time to enact them. So anyone who sees Parliament as a reliable guardian of human rights in practice is, I suggest, guilty of wishful thinking.

The second factor which gives the question a special immediacy is of quite a different nature. It is the increasingly heterogeneous nature of our society and the increasingly assertive stance of minorities. The inhabitants of these islands have never, of course, sprung from a pure common stock: Jutes, Angles, Saxons, Vikings, Normans, Huguenots and Jewish refugees from various parts of Europe are among those who have over the centuries blended with the native Celt and those indigenous Gael. But it is probably true that post-war immigration, particularly form the Indian subcontinent and the West Indies, has made us a more heterogeneous people than we have ever been. And it is surely true that some of these more recent citizens have shown less willingness to be submerged in the prevailing British way of life, and more desire to preserve their own traditions of language, customs, and religion, than most of their predecessors have been inclined to do. There is at the same time a general lessening of deference towards author-ity, a growing unwillingness to accept the say-so of the teacher, the local government officer, or the man from the ministry. So it seems reasonable to predict a growing number of cases—not only involving the ethnic minori-ties, but very often involving some minority—in which prevailing practice, perhaps of very long standing, will be said to infringe the human rights of some smaller ground or some individual. As it stands, our courts are not well-fitted to mediate in these situations.

Those who share my view that the situation is unsatisfactory may well ask whether it is nonetheless inevitable, one of those inescapable blemishes which must exist in an imperfect world. I would say not. In the European Convention an instrument lies ready to hand which, if not providing an ideal solution, nonetheless offers a clear improvement on the present position.

The History of the European Convention

I hope I may be permitted to touch on the history of the Convention, as I shall now call it, with apologies to those already very familiar with these points and with gratitude to Lord Lester QC, from whose work most of them are drawn.[5]

First, the Convention was not (as might have been thought) the ethereal brainchild of some continental professor. It was in large part prepared by British lawyers and in particular by that most terrestrial of politicians, the late Lord Kilmuir.[6] Its main protagonists in the early stages were Churchill, Macmillan, and John Foster, with Liberal and some Labour support.

Secondly, during the antenatal stages of the Convention the focus of discussion was not the substance of the rights themselves, which was thought to be rather obvious, but the means of enforcement, a matter of some understandable difficulty.

Thirdly, despite the British contribution to siring the Convention, the United Kingdom's ratification of it was fraught with dissension. Although

---

[5] Lester, see above n. 2, at p. 46.
[6] R. F. V. Heuston, *Lives of the Lord Chancellors 1940–1970* (1987), p. 166.

supported by Ernest Bevin, the Foreign Secretary, ratification was strongly opposed by the Chancellor of the Exchequer (Cripps), the Colonial Secretary (Griffiths) and, in particular, the Lord Chancellor (Jowitt), who reported to a colleague that the cabinet

were not prepared to encourage our European friends to jeopardise our whole system of law, which we have laboriously built up over the centuries, in favour of some half-baked scheme to be administered by some unknown court.[7]

He also described the proposed Commission on Human Rights as 'a sort of Court of Star Chamber'. Sir Hartley Shawcross, the Attorney-General, was similarly of the view that

we should firmly set our faces against the right of individual petition which seems to me to be wholly opposed to the theory of responsible Government.

Only at Bevin's insistence did the United Kingdom continue to support the Convention, and then only on the clear understanding that the United Kingdom Government could not accept the right of individual petition and the proposed European Court of Human Rights, nor various amendments which had been proposed.

Fourthly, subject to these reservations the United Kingdom did sign the Convention and, on 8 March 1951, (the day before Bevin's replacement by Herbert Morrison), became the first state to ratify. But with no incorporation into United Kingdom law, no right of individual petition and no recognition of the compulsory jurisdiction of the Strasbourg Court, the Convention was—to the United Kingdom—a hobbled horse. And when in October 1951 a Conservative government was returned to power, nothing was done to fulfil the ambitions of the Convention's founding fathers. When the Minister of State for Foreign Affairs was asked in 1958 what was the good of ratifying the Convention if one did not accept its application he answered:

As I understand it, if one subscribes to a Convention one then sees that the laws of one's country are in conformity with the Convention, and the individual cases are then tried under the laws of one's own country.[8]

But he might of course have added that the laws of one's own country may not necessarily conform with the Convention until the citizen has been put to the trouble and expense of going to Strasbourg to procure that result.

Fifthly, it was not until December 1965—after, but not immediately after, the election of a Labour government—that the decision was made to accept for a limited period the right of individual petition to the Commission and

---

[7] Interestingly, however, Jowitt does seem to have assumed that the Convention would have to be incorporated into domestic law: Lester, see above n. 2, at p. 53.

[8] Lester, see above n. 2, at p. 59.

the compulsory jurisdiction of the Court. This momentous decision, so recently thought to jeopardize our whole system of law laboriously built up over centuries, and to undermine responsible government, was apparently taken without discussion by the Cabinet or any Cabinet committee.[9]

Sixthly, the years since that decision was taken have seen publication of a report by the Northern Ireland Standing Advisory Commission on Human Rights and a Lords Select Committee Report, both recommending incorporation, and two Bills having that object have completed all stages in the Lords. Support has come from such distinguished and politically diverse quarters as Lord Hailsham, Lord Gardiner, Lord Scarman, and Lord Jenkins of Hillhead.

Meanwhile, seventhly and lastly, on an ever-lengthening list of occasions, many of them well-publicized, the Commission or the Court have found the United Kingdom to be in breach of its obligations under the Convention. Her Majesty's Government has, as one would expect, responded appropriately by taking steps to cure the default and pay compensation where indicated. These breaches have been established on individual petition by the aggrieved citizens, who before applying are obliged to exhaust their remedies here. The whole process is one which takes a very long time and costs a great deal of money. And the problem is getting worse. On 12 October 1992, the Strasbourg Court gave judgment in four cases. In those cases, the total length of time which proceedings took before the Commission and the Court was four years and six months, six years and eight months, six years and nine months, and seven years an one month.[10] The Strasbourg machine is becoming overwhelmed by the burdens placed upon it. But despite unremitting argument over the last few years that the Convention should be incorporated into English law so as to make its provisions enforceable, like every other law, by judges sitting in this country, no governmental move has been made in that direction.

The Argument for and Against Incorporation

Since incorporation would seem, at first blush, to be a simple and obvious way not only of honouring the United Kingdom's international obligations but also of giving direct and relatively inexpensive protection to its citizens, one would suppose that very powerful reasons must exist for not taking this step. It is indeed true that over the years a number of arguments against incorporation have been powerfully and persistently put. I shall review what I believe to be the more important of these arguments.

[9] Lester, see above n. 2, at p. 60.
[10] Andrew Drzemczewski, 'The Need for a Radical Overhaul' (1993) 143 N.L.J. 126.

Constitutional experts point out, first of all, that the unwritten British constitution, unlike virtually every written constitution, has no means of entrenching, that is of giving a higher or trump-like status to a law of this kind. Therefore, it is said, what one sovereign Parliament enacts another sovereign Parliament may override: thus a government minded to under-mine human rights could revoke the incorporation of the Convention and leave the citizen no better off than he is now, and perhaps worse. I would give this argument beta for ingenuity and gamma, or perhaps omega, for political nous. It is true that in theory any Act of Parliament may be repealed. Thus theoretically the legislation extending the vote to the adult population, or giving the vote to women, or allowing married women to own property in their own right, or forbidding cruel and unusual punish-ment, or safeguarding the independence of the judges, or providing for our adhesion to the European Community, could be revoked at the whim of a temporary parliamentary majority. But absent something approaching a revolution in our society such repeal would be unthinkable. Why? Because whatever their theoretical status constitutional measures of this kind are in practice regarded as enjoying a peculiar sanctity buttressed by overwhelm-ing public support. If incorporated, the Convention would take its place at the head of this favoured list. There is a second reason why formal en-trenchment is not necessary. Suppose the statute of incorporation were to provide that subject to any express abrogation or derogation in any later statute the rights specified in the Convention were to be fully recognised and enforced in the United Kingdom according to the tenor of the Conven-tion. That would be good enough for the judges. They would give full effect to the Convention rights unless a later statute very explicitly and specifically told them not to . But the rights protected by the Convention are not stated in absolute terms: there are provisos to cover pressing considerations of national security and such like. Save in quite extraordinary circumstances one cannot imagine any government going to Parliament with a proposal that any human right guaranteed by the Convention be overridden. And even then (subject to any relevant derogation) the United Kingdom would in any event remain bound, in international law and also in honour, to comply with its Convention obligations. I find it hard to imagine a govern-ment going to Parliament with such a proposal. So while the argument on entrenchment has a superficial theoretical charm, it has in my opinion very little practical substance. There would be no question, as under Community law, of United Kingdom judges declaring United Kingdom statutes to be invalid. Judges would either comply with the express will of Parliament by construing all legislation in a manner consistent with the Convention. Or, in the scarcely imaginable case of an express abrogation or derogation by Parliament, the judges would give effect to that provision also.

A second and quite different argument runs roughly along the following lines. Rulings on human rights, not least rulings on the lines of demarcation between one right and another, involve sensitive judgments important to individual citizens and to society as a whole. These are not judgments which unelected English (or perhaps British) judges are fitted to make, drawn as they are from a narrow, unrepresentative minority, the public-school and Oxbridge-educated, male, white, mostly protestant, mostly middle-class, products of the Bar. They are judgments of an essentially political nature, properly to be made by democratically elected representatives of the people. I do not, surprisingly, agree with most of the criticisms which it is fashionable to direct at the composition of the modern judiciary. Nor would I, again surprisingly, accept the charge sometimes made that protection of human rights cannot safely be entrusted to British judges: no one familiar with the development of the law in fields as diverse as, for example, the Rent Acts, the Factories Act, labour law, or judicial review could, I think, fairly accuse the judges of throwing their weight on the side of the big battalions against the small man or woman. But it is true that judgments on human rights do involve judgments about relations between the individual and the society of which the individual is part, and in that sense they can be described as political. If such questions are thought to be inappropriate for decisions by judges, so be it. I do not agree, but I can understand the argument. What I simply do not understand is how it can be sensible to entrust the decision of these questions to an international panel of judges in Strasbourg—some of them drawn from societies markedly unlike our own—but not, in the first instance, to our own judges here. I am not suggesting that the final right of appeal to Strasbourg should be eliminated or in any way curtailed (which, indeed, is not something which most opponents of incorporation support). I am only suggesting that rights claimed under the Convention should, in the first place, be ruled upon by judges here before, if regrettably necessary, appeal is made to Strasbourg. The choice is not between judges and no judges; it is whether *all* matches in this field must be played away.

The proposition that judgments on questions of human rights are, in the sense indicated, political is relied on by opponents of incorporation to found a further argument. The argument is that if British judges were to rule on questions arising under the Convention they would ineluctably be drawn into political controversy with consequent damage to their reputation, constitutionally important as it is, for political neutrality. This argument, espoused by a number of senior and respected political figures, should not be lightly dismissed. But it should be examined. It cannot in my view withstand such examination for two main reasons. The first is that judges are already, on a regular and day-by-day basis, reviewing and often quashing decisions of ministers and government departments. They have been doing so on an increasing scale for thirty years. During that period ministers of both governing parties have fallen foul of court decisions, not once or twice but repeatedly. Some of these decisions have achieved great public notoriety. All judges are accustomed to making every effort to put aside their own personal viewpoints, and there is no reason to think that English judges are any less good at this than any others. Political controversy there has been, on occasion, a-plenty, but it has not by and large rubbed off on the judges. Why not? Because, I think, it is generally if not universally recognized that the judges have a job to do, which is not a political job, and their personal predilections have no more influence on their decisions than that of a boxing referee who is required to stop a fight. In a mature democracy like ours, this degree of understanding is not, surely, surprising, but it does in my view weaken in this argument against incorporation.

There is, I suggest, a second reason why this is not a good argument. Although there are states other than the United Kingdom which have not incorporated the Convention into their domestic law, in particular the Scandinavian countries, most parties of the Convention have done so. Thus the judges of Austria, Switzerland, Italy, Belgium, Cyprus, France, Greece, Luxembourg, the Netherlands, Portugal, Spain, Turkey, Germany, Liechtenstein, and elsewhere give effect to the Convention as part of their own domestic law. If doing so involves them in political controversy damaging to their judicial role one would expect to find evidence of that unhappy result. There is to my knowledge no such evidence, and I do not think that those who advance this argument have ever pointed to any.

An additional argument sometimes heard is that incorporation is unnecessary since the Convention rights are already protected by the common law. The House of Lords recently held that in the field of freedom of speech there is no difference in principle between English law and Article 10 of the Convention.[11] Lord Goff of Chieveley said the same thing in one of the *Spycatcher* judgments.[12] But the House of Lords' earlier *Spycatcher* decision[13] has itself been held to have violated the Convention, as of course have other of their Lordships' decisions. If in truth the common law as it stands were giving the rights of United Kingdom citizens the same protection as the Convention—across the board, not only in relation to Article 10—one might wonder why the United Kingdom's record as a Strasbourg litigant was not more favourable.

There are those who argue against incorporation on the grounds that to do so would give permanent form to a view of society and the human

[11] *Derbyshire County Council* v. *Times Newspapers Ltd.* [1993] 2 WLR 449.
[12] *Att.-Gen.* v. *Guardian Newspapers Ltd. (No. 2)* [1990] 1 AC 109 at pp. 283–4.
[13] [1987] 1 WLR 1248.

condition which, though accepted immediately post-war at the time of drafting, has no claim to eternal verity. Further, it is said, a constraint is placed on the ability of the law to develop and change as the views of society develop and change. This is, in truth, an argument against the Convention itself. But it is not a very persuasive argument, since the Convention can of course by modified to reflect changing views and values. And there is a more fundamental answer, which is to look, necessarily very briefly, at the rights which the Convention (including its First Protocol) protects.

The rights (shorn of very important qualification) are: the right to life; the right to protection against subjection to torture or inhuman or degrading treatment or punishment; the prohibition of slavery and forced labour; the liberty and security of the person; the right to a fair trial; the prohibition of retrospective criminal legislation; the right to respect for private and family life, home, and correspondence; the right to freedom of thought, conscience and religion; the right to freedom of expression; the right to freedom of peaceful assembly and association; the right to marry and found a family; the right to peaceful enjoyment of property; the right to education; the requirement that there be free elections at reasonable intervals by secret ballot; and the right to enjoy these rights and freedoms without discrimination on any ground.

Now it is obvious that the content of these rights will be held to change as social and political attitudes develop. This has demonstrably happened already. For example, punishments which were commonplace (at least in the United Kingdom) in 1950 have been held to be, and would now be very widely thought to be, degrading. Views are bound to change on what the Articles of the Convention require and, not less important, what the qualifications to the Articles permit. I cannot, however, for my part accept that these Articles represent some transient sociological mood, some flavour of the month, the decade, or the half-century. They encapsulate legal, ethical, social, and democratic principles, painfully developed over 2,000 years. The risk that they may come to be regarded as modish or *passé* is one that may safely be taken.

I am conscious that I have given much time to considering the arguments against incorporation and rather less to the case in favour. this is no doubt because I regard the positive case as clear and the burden as lying on the opponents to make good their grounds of opposition. But there is one argument in favour of incorporation that I would like to mention. It is not a new argument,[14] but it is an important one, and it has recently been drawn to the House of Lords' attention by Lord Slynn of Hadley (in his legislative, and not his judicial, mode).[15] The Court of Justice has now made clear that

[14] See, e.g. Andrew Drzemczewski, *The European Human Rights Convention in Domestic Law* (1983), Ch. 9, p. 229.
[15] HL Deb., 26 November 1992, cols. 1096–1098.

the fundamental human rights which the Convention protects are part of the law of the Community which that court is bound to secure and enforce. Community law is, of course, part of the law of the United Kingdom. As Lord Slynn put it,

every time the European court recognises a principle set out in the convention as being part of Community law, it must be enforced in the United Kingdom courts in relation to Community law matters, but not in domestic law. So the convention becomes in part a part of our law through the back door because we have to apply the convention in respect of Community law matters as a part of Community law.

Drawing on his own experience as counsel appearing at Strasbourg he felt it would be more satisfactory if the convention were to enter by the front door. It was, he said

quite plain that many, although perhaps not all, of the cases could be dealt with just as well and more expeditiously by our won judges here.

Conclusion

I end on a downbeat note. It would be naive to suppose that incorporation of the Convention would usher in the new Jerusalem. As on the morrow of a general election, however glamorous the promises of the campaign, the world would not at once feel very different. But the change would over time stifle the insidious and damaging belief that it is necessary to go abroad to obtain justice. It would restore this country to its former place as an international standard-bearer of liberty and justice.It would help to reinvigorate the faith, which our eighteenth and nineteenth century forbears would not for an instant have doubted, that these were fields in which Britain was the world's teacher, not its pupil. And it would enable the judges more effectively to honour their ancient and sacred undertaking to do right to all manner of people after the laws and usages of their realm, without fear or favour, affection or ill will.

2

Rights and Rites for a New Britain

ANDREW MARR[1]

Do we need a British Bill of Rights, which is not merely the Britification of the European rights legislation, as persuasively advocated by Lord Lester QC, the Labour Party, and others? Incorporating into British law our longstanding adherence to the European Convention on Human Rights makes legal sense. It would be convenient, saving numerous trips to the continent. On those occasions when rights-based cases could then be resolved by courts here, not there, it would calm the easily-aroused ire of Britannic xenophobes about foreign judges. It would save money. Finally, it would be honest, openly admitting that the increased power of the judiciary in such cases was here to stay and was acceptable, and not some hideous alien growth on the pure native stock of parliamentary absolutism.

Here, though, I want to look both further back at the origins of rights-based politics, and also further ahead at the future of the 'rights agenda' in Britain. Do we need more? To talk of rights implies a contract, either between individuals or between citizen and state. In the *ancien regime* of European monarchy, where political involvement was tightly restricted and the application of law was arbitrary, it was comparatively easy for the French *philosophes* and revolutionary writers like Tom Paine to articulate a code of basic legal and political entitlements. But what was the deeper contract they were drawing on? It was an irony that so many of the early advocates of the rights of man were atheists, given that their ideology would have been impossible (so I judge) without the Christian teaching that all sinners are equal before God and that individuals owed one another duties of charity, pity, and so on. But it wasn't an enormous leap of imagination to suggest that men (and later women) ought therefore to be equal before the law too, and equal in their ability to influence the making of laws through democratic choice.

[1] Andrew Marr is the editor of *The Independent*.

The Origin of Human Rights

The cult of the noble savage and a widespread belief that mankind was once naked, innocent and possessed of natural rights may have been woolly but it acted as a bridge between religious egalitarianism and politics. It implied a pre-existing, unwritten, universal social contract by which individuals owed one another particular consideration; when this was violated, as by royal absolutism or despotic laws, nature was affronted. Paine wrote: 'Every civil right grows out of a natural right . . .' As science continued to advance and the bloodiness of the natural struggle for survival impressed itself on intellectual life, this lumping together of nobility, savages, nature, and jurisprudence seemed increasingly odd. Jeremy Bentham, that hard-headed man, and a jurist, found that 'Natural rights is simple nonsense: natural and imprescriptible rights, rhetorical nonsense—nonsense upon stilts'. Samuel Coleridge, in his splenetic old age, fully agreed: 'Rights! There are no rights whatever without corresponding duties . . . you will find nowhere in our parliamentary records the miserable sophism of the Rights of Man'.

The triumph of liberalism, based on the needs of industrial revolution and urbanization ensured that public opinion, on this issue at least, was more with Paine than Coleridge. That there are natural rights may be biological nonsense; but it became an unquestioned and necessary nonsense. Enlightenment led to the cult of the rights of man, and thus to revolution; and eventually, as the masses pressed closer, to a belief in political equality. There were many backwaters, stagnant pools, and counter-currents; but that was the broad stream of advance in rights-based thinking. Legal equality had been more practised in England than France or Germany; Scotland, as a presbyterian nation, had an earlier proto-democratic religious culture still. Political rights for Jews, Catholics, and dissenters were controversial through Victoria's reign. In revolutionary America, where Paine was a hero and his books very widely read, the idea of full democratic rights was nevertheless considered abhorrent by the leading statesmen who forged the new nation. Among the bourgeois and aristocratic leaders of the nineteenth century, a theoretical belief in human rights made way only slowly against their fear of the working-classes and their prejudice against female capacity. Rights for women may have been raised as a slogan by Mary Wollstonecraft more than 200 years ago; but it took over a century for these rights to be won. Indeed, because of the slow advance of the female franchise, Britain cannot be properly considered a democracy until the late 1920s. Nevertheless, it is not necessary to be a rosy-spectacled progressive to detect the current reaching from philosophical enlightenment in the 1770s to the European Court of Human Rights today. That current has not reached its logical end-point advance in Britain until we have an incorporated Bill of Rights. It isn't a matter of giving judges too many powers. The Enlightenment belief in inalienable rights, woolly or not, is clearly incompatible with Parliamentary absolutism, which is a residue not of the English revolution, but of many centuries of despotism. Tom Paine's work has not been completed in his native land. On the centre-left of politics this is now pretty close to being a matter of consensus.

The Extension of Rights

If rights-based politics stopped there, we could anticipate the conclusion of a long struggle—not the end of History, perhaps, but one successful part of the liberal project finally accomplished by a Blair administration. But rights are not so easily limited. Their allure spreads and spreads. Though the classical liberal position rests on a division between political/legal rights (good) and economic or social rights (bad), the separation has never been as easy as that. The radical wing of the parliamentary army during the English Civil War, which threw up some of the first democratic politicians these islands have known, assumed that without land rights there could be no political rights. Gerard Winstanley and his Diggers set at St George's Hill in Surrey with hoes and mattocks as an earthy assertion of their political, human rights. Tom Paine himself included a fairly detailed proposal for pensions and rudimentary welfare in his *Rights of Man*. The Marxist and socialist tradition has never recognised the validity of political rights without economic rights; indeed it has often raised economic rights over the other kind, with disastrous consequences. During the last years of the previous century and throughout this one, the right of organized labour to combine has become enmeshed into earlier lists of rights. Few people today would deny that the right not to starve, and to have a roof is as real and fundamental a right as the right to vote or the right to a fair trial.

The idea of economic or welfare rights is now strongly entrenched in the minds of many voters and is just beginning to spread to the political debate. During the 1995 Liberal Democrat conference in Glasgow, one of the leading activists in the campaign for a Scottish Parliament was addressing a late-night meeting and raised the idea of a Scottish Bill of Rights. One English lawyer in the audience queried the need for this, as compared with a merely British one. He was told that the Edinburgh version would give Scots the next bundle of inalienable rights, such as the right to free health care, free education, a job, benefits, and so on. Nor do the new politics of rights stop with economic rights. The right to control of one's fertility; the right not to be sexually harrassed; the right to live in a relatively unpolluted environment; the right to privacy; the right of children not be smacked . . . all would be the subject of amendments to any contemporary British Bill of

Rights legislation. At the further end of the spreading spectrum, there are the rights of future generations to be considered and even animal rights. Philosophers such as Peter Singer, the Australian who invented the concept of animal liberation, have argued that the circle of responsibility and rights now needs to be widened to the great apes, then other vertebrates and so on. One day 'species-ism' will be regarded as just as heinous a sin as sexism or racism. Rights, in short, seem almost as limitless as human wants. To describe all this as a politics of rights, going far ahead of any actual Bill of Rights, is all very well. But many of the above rights, however new and however they may conflict with other asserted rights, abortion being an obvious example, are now felt by voters as being real rights, as important as conventional political rights. Here Enlightenment Man, well-meaning, conventional, tidy-minded, pauses aghast, tips his wig back over his perspiring pate and asks that most of the above 'be not heard' (as they say in the House of Lords).

Principles of Inclusion

Pollution, sexual harrassment and identity, racism, rights of shelter, and rights to health care are all acknowledged as fit subjects for legal complaint and political argument. They are all part of the perpetual negotiation that is politics. They are our daily business. The question is which of them, if any, should be given the special status of inclusion in a Bill of Rights. Short of a political revolution which transformed its status and remade our leading institutions (which may be welcome but is not imminent) any Parliament would be able in due course to remove rights from some such list. But it would be difficult, and presumably unpopular. There are, I believe, three principles which could be used to limit demands for enshrined rights. The first is consensus. A Bill of Rights is in essence a statement of a society's fundamental principles. These change but only slowly. Such a list should be more of a fall-back in times of perplexity and trouble than a way of driving forward social advance. A proposed additional right which a significant proportion of people fiercely oppose may be a good idea and may be a fit subject for ordinary legislation and legal challenge; but it is not firmly accepted enough to reach a bill of rights. On this basis, the 'right to life' or the right to free abortion on demand would not be included; but possibly the right to free health care, or housing, could be. The rights of animals not to be eaten, or children not to be smacked, may come one day; but they are a very long way from being the sort of consensual basic value on which British life rests today. More immediately, proposed new rights which obviously conflicted with the beliefs of major religious groups, would instantly be signalled as dangerous and set aside.

The second principle would be that the rights so enshrined must be practical, which includes affordable. The right to a minimum level of income, sufficient to sustain a decent level of life, could be included. (But what does decent mean?) Equally clearly, the right to an interesting, well-paid job, or to freedom from onerous taxation, could not be included. These are things for politicians to argue about and strive for. The right not to suffer from the effects of pollution is also wholly impractical in a busy, noisy, car-obsessed, and materially rich culture such as our own. It may be a fit subject for campaigning and political argument; but taken literally (as a Bill of Rights is meant to be taken) it isn't a practical proposition.

The third principle is that wider rights must be not only consensual and practical but also clear. It is of course the case that the meaning of current entitlements under the European Convention is often fuzzy; otherwise there would be very few such cases and they would be over quickly. Some rights, such as the right not to be tortured, are clear enough. But the right to freedom of speech is one which is bound to be subject to continual negotiation and argument, partly because it conflicts with other laws, for instance on obscenity and racism. Even so, any new social, political, or moral right which was vague enough to cause a frown at first sight would diminish the whole concept of a special category of rights. If there are to be special, perimeter-setting rules for social behaviour, then they have to be rules the average voter can instantly understand and, mostly, assent to.

If these three principles are respected, I can see no legitimate or logical reason to limit the extension of a British Bill of Rights to narrowly-defined political or legal rights. Common sense indicates that such a Bill cannot be very long, simply because quite soon asserted rights start to clash and therefore become meaningless. But if the American Bill of Rights was intended to set out that society's guiding principles of individual freedom and respect, there is no reason why later, more welfarist and perhaps more squeamish societies should not codify and elevate different rules. Notwithstanding Francis Fukuyama, The Enlightenment did not set the rules for all people and for all time; nor was it enlightened about everything.

Rights and Duties

There is one final proposal, however, which I suggest deserves consideration when and if British politicians decide to go beyond the relatively safe waters of current human rights legislation. We should return, as fashionable sociologists everywhere suggest, to Coleridge's point about there being no rights without 'corresponding duties'. If a Bill of Rights is intended as a part-practical, part-symbolic expression of what the badge of citizenship brings with it, then there is a strong case for making this a double-sided contract. Most rights are already legal obligations of one sort or another elsewhere; the bill of rights is there mainly to distinguish them as particularly important. Similarly, though our basic civil obligations as taxpayers, parents, neighbours and so on are all present in English or Scottish law, there is a case for enshrining them in the same contract as our rights. The duty of obeying laws; the duty of care for children or elderly relatives; the tax-paying duty; the duty to respect others' rights . . . all these are currently clear enough. But in a society lacking clear moral direction and apparently plagued by uncertainty, it might be a useful act to append such duties to a new Bill of Rights. New voters might even be required to sign such a contract—not with the State, but with their fellow-citizens. Every society needs rituals of belonging and responsibility; these days we have few of them left and such a coming-of-age event might be a useful novelty—new rites to go with new rights.

3

Why We Need a Constitutional Court

RICHARD GORDON QC

Introduction

There are many compelling reasons why the European Convention on Human Rights should be incorporated into domestic law. One of the most compelling is, however, one of the least articulated. It is that modern judicial review, the citizen's constitutional safeguard, in fact lacks any respectable constitutional dimension for the protection of human rights. More accurately, it is that the jurisdictional basis on which judicial review is exercised so as to effect protection of human rights is almost exclusively dependent upon the formulation, by the judges, of *administrative* law principles. These principles, however, derive their existence not from any constitutional underpinning but from the incremental nature of the common law in general and from judicial creativity in particular.

It is sometimes asserted that there is no constitutional axis for judicial review at all. Certainly, the extension of the boundaries of judicial review to cover non-statutory bodies and the use of prerogative powers[1] could have occurred only as the consequence of an open-ended source of law-making authority in the judges rather than from scrutiny of power conferred by the legislature.

None the less the vice, at least in the area of human rights, is self-evident. If the parameters of judicial review in this area are constrained, principally, by the limits that the judges choose to place on the development of legal principle it follows that an individual's 'human rights', howsoever those are to be defined, are virtually co-extensive with judicial fiat.

For different reasons, and no doubt for different ends, there are now many who seek to curb the powers of the judges.[2] But this entails a further consequence even more stark than the supposed terrors of judicial absolutism. Without a constitutional foundation for the protection of human rights

---

[1] For the development of this see Wade & Forsyth *Administrative Law* (7th ed., 1994) at pp. 659–67.

[2] For an invocation to judicial self-restraint see 'Judges and Decision-Makers: The Theory and Practice of *Wednesbury* Review', Lord Irvine of Lairg Q.C. (1996) PL 59.

every limitation on the power of the courts to overturn executive excess becomes a potential threat to liberty, freedom, and the individual.

The undoubted tension that currently subsists between powers that should, consistent with Diceyan constitutional thinking, be separate[3] is itself the product of a failure to establish a constitutional basis for human rights. If the United Kingdom were to incorporate the European Convention on Human Rights and to create a constitutional court for its implementation there would be diminished scope for conflict between the executive and the judges. The latter would be restrained by the powers conferred by the former.

Lack of a Constitutional Basis for Human Rights

The bedrock of judicial review is said to be the doctrine of *ultra vires*.[4] Essentially, this permits judicial intervention so as to ensure that powers conferred by the legislature are not exercised contrary to their intended statutory purpose.

This is the rationale for the refusal of the courts to deploy the European Convention on Human Rights to imply an automatic intention by the legislature to act consistently with it. In *R* v. *Secretary of State for the Home Department*, ex p. *Brind*[5] the House of Lords clarified that the utility of the Convention is, in this context, merely to resolve an ambiguity in primary or subordinate legislation. Were the position otherwise Parliamentary Sovereignty would be impugned since it must be open to Parliament to legislate contrary to a Convention that is, as yet, unincorporated.

It is deeply unattractive that the premise upon which *ultra vires* depends for its existence is one that, if applied, could allow the reality of liberty to be eroded so as to preserve the analytic integrity of the principle. In fact, as will be seen, this is not what happens. But it only fails to happen because of the judges' tacit abandonment of *ultra vires* where there is a danger of collision between human rights on the one hand and legal principle on the other.

Judicial Treatment of Human Rights

Notwithstanding the decision on *Brind*, judges undertaking judicial review have found ways of ameliorating its effect. Two examples outlined here

---

[3] See A. V. Dicey 'Introduction to the Study of the Law of the Constitution' (1st ed., 1885).
[4] Sir William Wade describes it as 'the central principle of administrative law': see Wade & Forsyth, above n. 1, at p. 41.
[5] [1991] AC 696.

serve to demonstrate that the techniques utilized depend on administrative law powers and not on an application of *ultra vires*.

In *R* v. *Secretary of State for the Home Department*, ex p. *McQuillan*[6] Sedley J developed the notion that where a breach of a fundamental right is in issue, a higher standard of justification is required than would, otherwise, be the case. He said this:

Once it is accepted that the standards articulated in the European Convention are standards which both march with those of the common law and inform the jurisprudence of the European Union, it becomes unreal and potentially unjust to continue to develop English public law without reference to them. Accordingly, and without in any way departing from the ratio decidendi of *ex parte Brind*, the legal standards by which the decisions of public bodies are supervised can and should differentiate between those rights which are regarded as fundamental, and those which, though known to the law, do not enjoy such a pre-eminent status. Once this point is reached, the standard of justification of infringements of rights and freedoms by executive decision must vary in proportion to the significance of the right which is at issue . . . Whether this is in itself a doctrine of proportionality, I do not now pause to ask. If it is, then the House of Lords has long since contemplated its arrival with equanimity.

So, too, in *R* v. *Ministry of Defence*, ex p. *Smith and Others*[7] the Court of Appeal, whilst ostensibly re-stating the traditional *ultra vires* basis for judicial review, pointed the way to a heightened review process in the case of fundamental human rights. Sir Thomas Bingham MR accepted Counsel's submission that:

The court may not interfere with the exercise of an administrative discretion on substantive grounds save where the court is satisfied that the decision is unreasonable in the sense that it is beyond the range of responses open to a reasonable decision-maker. But in judging whether the decision-maker has exceeded this margin of appreciation the human rights context is important. The more substantial the interference with human rights, the more the court will require by way of justification before it is satisfied that the decision is reasonable in the sense outlined above.

These and other[8] pronouncements suggest that where an important or 'fundamental' human right is at stake the courts will strive to accommodate such right by reference to open-ended administrative law principles such as the scope of the duty to give reasons[9] and not by recourse to the *ultra vires* doctrine.

---

[6] [1995] 4 All ER 400 at p. 422.

[7] [1996] 1 All ER 257 at p. 263d.

[8] See, e.g., the comments of Laws J. in *R* v. *Cambridge District Health Authority*, ex p. *B* (1995) *The Times*, March 15.

[9] Ex p. *Matson* (1996) 8 Admin L.R. 49 at p. 62B–D and 64B.

That principles of modern judicial review are, in part, derived from common law rather than from a consideration of what the legislature expressly or impliedly intended is exemplified by cases such as *Cooper* v. *Wandsworth Board of Works*.[10] There, an Act of Parliament stipulated that no one might erect a building in London without prior notice to the local board of works. Failure to give such notice gave the board the right to have the building demolished. When a builder failed to give the requisite notice and the board demolished the building it was, nonetheless, held that an action for damages lay. As Byles J observed:

although there are no positive words in a statute, requiring that the party shall be heard, yet the justice of the common law will supply the omission of the legislature.

In these cases it is the 'omission of the legislature' which, in the name of principles such as entitlement to procedural propriety or natural justice, the courts remedy by way of judicial review. But, this being so, *ultra vires* can never engage since the legislature cannot sensibly be said to have impliedly conferred powers which it has simply omitted to consider.

Similarly, judicial review of non-statutory entities such as the Panel on Take-Overs and Mergers or the Advertising Standards Authority[11] reflects the protection of the common law over abuse of a monopolistic position rather than application of the *ultra vires* principle.[12] This must be so given the absence of any legislative power whatever being exercised by such bodies. The insistence by the courts that, for susceptibility to judicial review of a non-statutory body, there must be an exercise of *governmental* power[13] is still wholly unconnected with *ultra vires* because, as the case law amply demonstrates, it is the nature of the *functions* rather than the *source* of the power which attracts the scrutiny of the court.

The reality is that the judges have consistently used their common law powers to protect what they see as the preservation of the rule of law. This is even so, perhaps especially so, where there is an ostensible conflict between *ultra vires* and the rule of law.

A striking example of this is afforded by the leading case of *Anisminic* v. *Foreign Compensation Commission*.[14] There, the House of Lords refused to uphold a statutory 'ouster' clause designed to remove the courts' control over determinations by the Foreign Compensation Commission. In commenting on the decision Professor Wade[15] observes as follows:

[10] (1863) 14 C.B. (NS) 180.
[11] See, e.g., *R* v. *Panel on Take Overs and Mergers*, ex p. *Datafin plc* [1987] QB 815; *R* v. *Advertising Standards Authority*, ex p. *The Insurance Service plc* (1990) COD 42.
[12] A point well made by C. Forsyth in 'Of Fig Leaves and Fairy Tales: The Ultra Vires Doctrine, the Sovereignty of Parliament and Judicial Review' (CLJ March 1996 p. 122).
[13] *R* v. *Disciplinary Committee of the Jockey Club*, ex p. *Aga Khan* [1993] 1 WLR 909.
[14] [1969] 2 A.C. 147.   [15] Wade and Forsyth, see above n. 1, at p. 737.

The object of the ouster clause in question ... was to keep the distribution of compensation outside the courts altogether ... The intention of Parliament was clear ... In refusing to enforce it the court was applying a presumption which may override even their constitutional obedience, namely that jurisdictional limits must be legally effective. This is tantamount to saying that judicial review is a constitutional fundamental which even the sovereign Parliament cannot abolish.

Thus, the reality appears to be that to the extent that the *ultra vires* principle fails to protect that which the courts regard as constitutionally essential, the judges will use the common law as a constitutional bulwark.

As Sir John Laws said in a recent paper:

[It] cannot be suggested that all these principles, which represent much of the bedrock of modern administrative law, were suddenly interwoven into the legislature's intentions in the 1960s and 70s and onward ... They are, categorically, judicial creations. They owe neither their existence nor their acceptance to the will of the legislature.[16]

This is a controversial stance and it is one that has, recently, come under severe attack.[17] Notably, however, the challenge to the view that judicial supremacism currently rules the roost in judicial review is based upon the express assertion that the doctrine of *ultra vires* affords a sufficient constitutional basis for what the judges are doing.[18]

If, as suggested here, it does not, then judicial activism becomes the citizen's sole protection against perceived misuse of executive power. It is, however, a most unsatisfactory protection both because the assertion of such a potentially unlimited jurisdiction creates inevitable tension between the legislature and the judiciary, and also because the methods by which the judges seek to invoke common law to protect 'fundamental' rights threaten to emasculate *ultra vires* altogether.

Put simply, if the judges are *de facto* responsible for protecting fundamental rights, they then have the correlative power of determining the limits of such rights. The judiciary, as the 'new barons', becomes, simply, the legislature in ermine. Not only is this unsatisfactory from a constitutional perspective; it is also dangerous from a human rights viewpoint.

Squaring the Circle

Properly analysed, the incorporation of the European Convention on Human Rights and the establishment of a Constitutional Court place *ultra vires* at the forefront of administrative law whilst, at the same time, making it both unnecessary and jurisdictionally impossible for judges to use

---

[16] 'Law and Democracy' [1995] Public Law 72 at p. 79. [17] See n. 2 above.
[18] See Wade and Forsyth above n. 1, see also n. 2.

uncircumscribed common law powers to trump some supposed constitutional deficiency.

This is, largely, what has occurred with European Union law. Section 2 of the European Communities Act 1972 is not an abdication of Parliamentary Sovereignty but is, rather, the ultimate assertion of the *ultra vires* doctrine. Our judges are neither free to ignore community law nor to seek to utilize common law as a residual yardstick of control. Indeed, where either statute or the common law is in conflict with European law, the former must be disapplied.

The view outlined here is that we need the clearest conferment by the legislature of fundamental rights coupled with a Constitutional Court where the power of the judges to give effect to those rights is precise and unequivocal. Without both there is a real danger that what is, currently, a constitutional tension may become a constitutional impasse. Even constitutional tension carries with it the prospect of untold harm to the fabric of administrative law in this country.

4

Why Incorporation of the European Convention on Human Rights is Not Enough

JOHN WADHAM[1]

The movement towards the incorporation of the European Convention of Human Rights into domestic law is gaining strength and this country remains one of the few in Europe which have not taken this step or already have some equivalent legislation. All of the major opposition parties have a policy of incorporation and if there is a change of government it is likely that this will actually happen. In this chapter I will argue that, although incorporation is a necessary and essential first step, the inadequacy of the contents of the Convention means that in order to properly protect rights in this country we need to create the mechanisms to draft and implement our own domestic Bill of Rights.[1]

Introduction

The history of the European Convention on Human Rights and Fundamental Freedoms goes back to before the establishment of the Council of Europe.[2] The Convention was partly based on the United Nations' Universal Declaration of Human Rights and the text of the Convention was finally agreed in 1950. The Convention is now 46 years old and that age is very apparent. Despite this (or perhaps because of this) the Convention is a 'living instrument' and the judges of the Court and the Commission have tried to ensure that changing standards in Europe are reflected in the decisions that they make. For instance, I am sure that in 1950 it was never envisaged that the right to privacy would allow the Court to hold that the criminal prosecution of adult gay men for consenting sexual intercourse was unlawful.[3]

---

[1] John Wadham is the Director of Liberty (formerly the National Council for Civil Liberties). Liberty has drafted such a Bill of Rights and the critique that follows is largely based on a comparison between that Bill and the Convention, see *People's Charter: Liberty's Bill of Rights*, Francesca Klug (Liberty, 1991).

[2] See, e.g., A. H. Robertson and J. G. Merrills. *Human Rights in Europe: A Study of the European Convention on Human Rights* (3rd ed., 1992).

[3] *Dudgeon* v. *UK*, 4 EHRR 149; *Norris* v. *Ireland*, 13 EHRR 186.

Nevertheless there are limits to how far this process can succeed in the long term and to how much the Contents of the Convention can be used to protect rights in the twenty-first century. None of the arguments that follow are reasons for not incorporating the Convention immediately or for denying the right of individuals to petition the European Commission or Court of Human Rights. The Convention must remain available to buttress a domestic Bill of Rights and to remain a remedy of last resort. Rather my argument is that we should have incorporated the Convention some twenty years or so ago.[4] Some of the faults in the Convention that I identify below could be remedied by the addition of new protocols to the Convention and this is something that could be actively pursued. Nevertheless there are very great obstacles to this project, not least of course, the need to obtain the consent of the more than thirty countries that are now members of the Council of Europe, the overwhelming majority of whom have signed up to the Convention.

Missing Rights

The Convention has a number of rights missing from its text which, I think, most people would now accept should be included.

(1) The Right to Know

There is no right to information from public bodies.[5] The right to information from personal files held by local authorities and the right to access to medical files have already been set out in statute in this country[6] and although their existence owes something to the Convention the cases in Strasbourg on freedom of information have only been successful as a corollary of other rights in the Convention, in particular, the right to privacy. The recent Code of Practice on Open Government[7] has no force in law and provides a very inadequate basis for a right to know.

This is not the place to set out the arguments for a right of freedom of information but I think that it is now clear that this right is very much overdue.

---

[4] In 1976 the International Covenant on Civil and Political Rights came into effect. More parochially, Liberty first articulated its policy on the incorporation of the Convention into domestic law based on publication by Liberty's sister organization, the Cobden Trust, in 1976 of *Civil Liberties and a Bill of Rights* by Peter Wallington and Jeremy McBride.

[5] Art. 10 only protects the right to impart information.

[6] Access to Medical Reports Act 1988, Access to Health Records Act 1990 and Access to Personal Files Act 1987.

[7] *'Open Government'* (HMSO, July 1993).

(2) The Rights of Immigrants, Asylum Seekers and Those Being Extradited

Under the Convention there is no duty on the State to provide rights of due process or to a fair trial in the extradition system or before deportation.[8] The rights contained in Article 6 of the Convention—the right to a fair trial—do not apply because the deportee has no pre-existing civil right to remain in this country and the right to a fair trial only applies where there is such a pre-existing right. One obvious and important right for those at risk of deportation would be a duty on the State seeking extradition to demonstrate a *prima facie* case in court before extradition was ordered.[9] Those extradited to other countries where they are likely to be far away from their friends and family and confronted by a foreign legal system conducted in a language they may not understand are at a considerable disadvantage and the State wishing to extradite them should, I suggest, only have the power to do so where the charge is serious, where there is sufficient evidence which, if proved, would be sufficient to convict them and where the trial system is patently fair.

The Convention also provides little assistance to those held in detention pending deportation or extradition because Article 5(1)(f) allows detention in such circumstances and there is apparently no limit to the length of detention nor any restriction on the merits of either the detention or the deportation.[10] In fact the rights of 'aliens' are further and specifically restricted by Article 16 which states that the rights of freedom of expression and assembly and the anti-discrimination Article shall not

be regarded as preventing the High Contracting Parties [the state] from imposing restrictions on the political activity of aliens.

The only restrictions on removal from a country are those imposed by other Articles such as the right to family life or freedom from torture.[11] Even in family life cases the Court has held[12] that if the family life can take place in

---

[8] The right to submit reasons, the right to review (not necessarily before a court) and the right to representation, before an expulsion is effected are contained in Protocol 7, Article 1 but this has not been ratified by the UK. The Article also permits expulsion without those protections where it 'is necessary in the interests of public order or is grounded on reasons of national security'.

[9] This was, of course, the position before the Criminal Justice Act 1988.

[10] Nevertheless in the case of *Chahal* v. *UK* (27 June 1995) Application No. 22414/93 the Commission has found a violation on the basis of the length of time Mr Chahal was detained pending deportation. This case is very special because the applicant has been detained for over five years pending deportation and the government's argument for deportation is based on claims of national security which were not specified in detail before the domestic courts.

[11] *Soering* v. *UK* (1989), EHRR 439. See also *Chahal* above.

[12] See *Abdulaziz, Cabales and Bakandali* v. *UK* (1985), 7 EHRR 471. It has taken particularly extreme circumstances for the Court to upheld a violation of the right to family life in such cases. For instance the Court decided that in a case of a person from Morocco convicted

the country to which the person is being deported then there is no breach of that Article.

Of course, the Convention does not includes the right to enter a country either as a resident or as an asylum seeker. Furthermore there is also no right to due process or to a fair trial for those who believe that they have substantive rights to enter and remain in the country. Even the rules giving a right to asylum in the United Nations Convention are not referred to in the European Convention.

(3) Anti-Discrimination Provisions

The right to be free from discrimination contained in Article 14 is flawed because, being drafted many years ago, it only deals with discrimination based on membership of some groups and does not refer for instance to a person's sexual orientation or disability.[13] It is also flawed because the freedom from discrimination provision only applies where, unlike for instance the United Nations International Covenant on Civil and Political Rights,[14] another right of the Convention has been violated. This has led to the provision being treated inadequately by the Commission and Court in Strasbourg, with them often preferring only to give judgment on the breach of the substantive right and ignoring Article 14.[15] This has left us with very little guidance on what Article 14 does mean but it is clear that at present it does not provided a proper basis to outlaw discrimination.

Thus Article 14 does not generally provide freedom from discrimination in jobs, services, or where a socio-economic right is at stake.

(4) Criminal Justice

In the context of minimum standards within the criminal justice system the Convention does not contain any equivalent of Article 14(3)(g) of the International Covenant on Civil and Political Rights. That is, that in the determination of any criminal charge, a person shall not 'be compelled to testify against himself or to confess guilt'.[16]

---

of a number of offences (none of them grave) and sentenced to 26 months imprisonment who had lived in Belgium since the age of three and all of whose close relatives including his parents, his seven brothers and sisters lived in Belgium the deportation was disproportionate *Moustaquim* v. *Belgium* 13 EHRR 802.

[13] However it does make unlawful discrimination based on 'other status'.

[14] See Art. 26.

[15] There are some important judgments however. See, e.g., the *Belgian Linguistic case* 1 EHRR 241.

[16] Although this may be partly protected. Two cases from the UK pending before the European Court of Human Rights may give guidance as to the extent to which the overall right to a fair trial contained in Art. 6(1) of the Convention and the presumption of innocence contained in Art. 6(2) protect the right to silence in criminal trials, see *Saunders* v. *UK* (10 May 1994), No. 19187/91 and *Murray* v. *UK* (27 June 1994), No. 18731/91.

The United Nations Human Rights Committee when considering the extent that provisions of the Criminal Justice and Public Order Act 1994, which makes substantial inroads into the right of silence, complied with the requirements of Article 14 said:

The Committee notes with concern that the provisions of the Criminal Justice and Public Order Act 1994 . . . whereby inferences may be drawn from the silence of persons accused of crimes, violates various provisions in article 14 of the Covenant, despite the range of safeguards built into the legislation and the rules enacted thereunder.[17]

Finally, the right to trial by jury in serious criminal cases is not contained anywhere in the Convention.[18]

(5) Detention

Although there are restrictions on the lawfulness of detention in the Convention no minimum conditions are set for conditions of detention outside those contained in Article 3—the provision against torture inhuman and degrading treatment or punishment.[19] The conditions required to breach the rights contained in Article 3 would have to be particularly severe and this provision is not designed to deal with 'merely inadequate' conditions of detention. Also other positive rights for those incarcerated are missing, in particular the right of access to a lawyer[20] and the right not to be held incommunicado.

(6) Privacy

The absence of any right of privacy in the United Kingdom means that for the purposes of Article 6, the right to a fair trial conducted by an independent court in any dispute concerning a *civil right*, does not exist in privacy cases. Thus the right to privacy is only protected to the extent of the

[17] July 1995.

[18] Such a right is also not contained in any other international treaty of human rights.

[19] See, e.g., the International Covenant on Civil and Political Rights, Art. 10(1), 'All persons deprived of their liberty shall be treated with humanity and with respect for the inherent dignity of the human person'.

[20] The right to access to a lawyer has of course been litigated in Strasbourg but only as a consequential effect of the right to correspondence and right to access to courts see, for instance, *Silver* v. *UK*, Series A, No. 61 and *Golder* v. *UK*, Series A, No. 18. These cases have not dealt with the right to see a solicitor on arrival at the police station as contained (in a less than perfect form) in s. 56 of the Police and Criminal Evidence Act 1984. In *Murray* v. *UK* (27 June 1994) No. 18731/91 the Commission has held that the failure to allow access within a reasonable period and the refusal to allow the lawyer to be present at police interviews breaches Art. 6. This is not a right in itself but is dependent on the fact that the evidence (including 'evidence' from the adverse inference consequent on the suspect's silence) which lead to the conviction may have resulted from the lawyers absence.

provisions in Article 8 itself. This means that, for instance, a compulsory search of someone's home or the forcible taking of bodily samples by the police does not have to be authorized by an independent court-like body but merely has to be 'in accordance with the law'. Rights of due process in relation to privacy are not required by the Convention. This has meant that the domestic telephone tapping[21] and security services tribunals[22] have been accepted by the Commission as providing sufficient protection.[23] This is despite the fact that there is no right to see any of the documents that the tribunal considers, no right to a hearing before the tribunal, no right for the tribunal to consider the actual merits of any surveillance and no right to challenge the decision of the tribunal in any court.

(7) *Other Rights*

Also absent from the Convention are any specific rights for children.[24]

Lastly it is important to realize that whilst some additional rights are contained in the protocols to the Convention most of these protocols have not been ratified by the United Kingdom and thus do not apply. Furthermore most of the attempts by parliamentarians to incorporate the Convention into domestic law have been restricted to incorporate only those rights which have been ratified, so that in addition to the rights of those about to be expelled from the country mentioned above other rights that are missing include: freedom from imprisonment for breach of contract,[25] freedom of movement and residence,[26] the right to appeal following conviction and the right of compensation for those wrongly convicted,[27] the prohibition on double jeopardy in criminal cases[28] and equality of rights between spouses.[29]

---

[21] Interception of Communications Act 1985.

[22] Security Services Act 1989 and Intelligent Services Act 1994.

[23] See respectively *Esbester* v. *UK* (2 April 1993) No. 18601/91 and *Christie* v. *UK* (27 June 1994) No. 21482/93. See also 'The Intelligence Services Act 1994' in *Modern Law Review*, Nov. 1994.

[24] Such as that contained in the International Covenant on Civil and Political Rights, Art. 24

1. Every child shall have, without any discrimination as to race, colour, sex, language, religion, national or social origin, property or birth, the right to such measures of protection as are required by his status as a minor, on the part of his family, society and the State.
2. Every child shall be registered immediately after birth and shall have a name.
3. Every child has the right to acquire a nationality.

[25] Protocol 4, Art. 1.

[26] Protocol 4, Art. 2.

[27] Protocol 7, Art. 2 and 3.

[28] Protocol 7, Art. 4.

[29] Protocol 7, Art. 5.

Content of the Convention

Apart from wholesale omissions of important rights there are considerable gaps and limitations in the rights as provided by the Convention. I will choose some of the more important of these to illustrate the problems.

Whilst the right to life contained in Article 2 is protected by the condition that actions breaching the right need to be 'absolutely necessary' the limitations include allowing lethal force to be used

(b) in order to effect a lawful arrest or to prevent the escape of a person lawfully detained;
(c) in action lawfully taken for the purpose of quelling a riot or insurrection.

I do not think that it can be right to allow the State to kill merely to effect an arrest or to prevent escape or even in order to end a riot.[30] Although it may be justified to kill in order to protect the lives of others where this is 'absolutely necessary'.

Article 5(1)(e) allows the

detention of persons for the prevention of the spreading of infectious diseases, of persons of unsound mind, alcoholics or drug addicts or vagrants.

Surely no one drafting a Bill of Rights today could include a right to imprison vagrants and alcoholics merely for what they are rather than for what they have done whatever differing views there may be of locking up those with infectious diseases?

The rights of privacy and the freedoms of religion, expression, and assembly are all subject to similar limitations in the Convention which are contained in the second part of the relevant Article:

except such as in accordance with the law and is necessary in a democratic society in the interests of national security, public safety or the economic well-being of the country, for the prevention of disorder or crime, for the protection of health or morals, or for the protection of the rights and freedoms of others.[31]

Whilst significant numbers of cases against the United Kingdom in Strasbourg have succeeded because the interference with the right was not 'in accordance with the law' or the interference was not proportionate—not 'necessary in a democratic society'—few have failed because the purported aim of the restriction was outside of the range provided for in the second part of the article. There is not space here to deal with all of the

---

[30] In the case of the shooting by members of SAS of three members of the IRA in Gibraltar the European Court of Human Rights decided, by a majority of 10 to 9, that the preparations and briefing of the soldiers was sufficiently inadequate to make the government liable for a breach of their right to life, *McCann* v. *UK*, 27 September 1995, Series A, No. 324.

[31] This is from Article 8(2), privacy and family life.

difficulties that the expression 'national security' creates for the courts[32] but it is arguable that the expression is too vague to be contained in a Bill of Rights.

Similarly the expression public safety makes too wide an exception and Liberty has substituted 'imminent physical harm' in its Bill of Rights.[33] Interestingly 'the economic well being of the country' features only as a limitation in Article 8, the right to privacy and not as a limitation for the freedoms of religion, expression, and assembly.

It is difficult to oppose the provision of a limitation based on the prevention of crime although Liberty's Bill of Rights avoids this altogether arguing that the 'protection of the rights and freedoms of others' is the only justifiable limitation that is necessary.

For similar reasons exceptions based on the prevention of disorder or the protection of health or morals are not only very vague but potentially unlimited in their effect and generally unacceptable as a limitation in themselves. As limitations on the rights of privacy and the freedoms of religion, expression, and assembly they are particularly problematic and, in my view, have no place in any Bill of Rights.

Article 12 of the Convention includes a right to marry and found a family but does not provide such a right for transsexuals.[34] It also, of course, only allows men and women to marry and makes no provision for partnerships between lesbians or between gay men.

One can certainly conclude from this brief analysis of the Convention that it is an inadequate basis for a Bill of Rights. A better foundation would be the International Covenant on Civil and Political Rights but better still would be a domestic Bill of Rights albeit based on such international treaties. Nevertheless the Convention should be incorporated into domestic law in the first year of the next government. Before even this is possible a few other issues need to be resolved.

Incorporation

In the challenge to the ban imposed by the Home Secretary on the media on broadcasts by members of Sinn Fein, the House of Lords took the view that

---

[32] See Lawrence Lustgarten and Ian Leigh, *In from the Cold: National Security and Parliamentary Democracy* (OUP, 1994). The courts have consistently refused to adjudicate in national security cases see *Council of Civil Service Unions* v. *Minister of the Civil Service* [1985] AC 374 or the refusal of the court to intervene in a claim for public interest immunity based on national security in a civil case *Balfour* v. *Foreign and Commonwealth Office* [1994] 2 All ER 588.

[33] See n. 1 above.

[34] *Rees* v. *UK*, Series A, No. 106 and *Cossey* v. *UK*, Series A, No. 184 but see the more recent decision on the rights of a transsexul parent *X, Y and Z* v. *UK*, June 27, 1995 No. 21830/93.

the Convention did not have to be taken into account by the executive arm of the State when such a wide-ranging discretion was being exercised.[35] This state of affairs could be overturned by statute and this would in fact be one of the effects of Lord Lester's Human Rights Bill which was designed to incorporate the Convention.[36] I think however that it is necessary to go much further than this and to use the statute incorporating the Convention[37] to overturn common law decisions that are in conflict with it, to ensure that subordinate legislation such as statutory instruments and orders in council are overturned to the extent that they conflict with the Convention and finally to create new rights by, for instance, a tort of breach of statutory duty thus ensuring that the Convention was a source of real law in itself. Similarly a breach of the Convention (rather just the failure to take it into account see *Brind*) could in itself found a decision of unlawfulness in judicial review proceedings.

In my view none of these options need breach any implied constitutional axiom of the sovereignty of Parliament. Traditional constitutional wisdom would say that all such changes, particularly those that bind a future Parliament, are impossible.[38] In fact the jurisprudence of the law of the European Union shows us that we can go further.[39] The courts are now obliged to strike down statute law which conflicts with the Treaty of Rome. I would wish to see a system modelled on the procedure in the Canadian Charter of Rights. In Canada whilst courts can overturn old and new legislation[40] which conflicts with the Charter the procedure also allows the legislature to declare *expressly* in an Act of Parliament that a given provision operates notwithstanding the Charter of rights. This 'notwithstanding clause' permits the Canadian Parliament to keep provisions on the statute book which the courts have overturned provided it is acknowledged that, in effect, they do not comply with the Charter.

---

[35] *Brind* v. *The Secretary of State for the Home Department* [1991] AC 696.

[36] House of Lords, 25 January 1995, col 1136; February 15 1995, col 762; 29 March 1995, col 1692 and 1 May 1995 col.

[37] I am use the Convention as an example it would be equally possible to have an alternative and I would say better basis for a Bill of Rights.

[38] '(that) Parliaments have more than once intended and endeavoured to pass Acts which should tie the hands of their successors is certain, but the endeavour has always ended in failure'. A. V. Dicey *Law of the Constitution*, p. 65. See by contrast A. W. Bradley, *The Sovereignty of Parliament—in Perpetuity* in *The Changing Constitution*, J. Jowell and D. Oliver (eds) (2nd ed., (1989)).

[39] *R* v. *Secretary of State for Transport* ex p. *Factortame* (*No. 2*) [1991] AC 603 ECJ.

[40] Ordinarily a 'chronologically superior' Act would take precedence in the case of conflict; *Ellen Street Estates* v. *Liverpool Corporation* [1932] 1 KB 733.

Litigants

The Convention currently allows both individuals, organizations and companies to take advantages of the rights that are contained within it. Now obviously some rights are only relevant to individuals and for instance it is not possible to imprison or torture a company. Nevertheless a considerable number of cases taken to the Commission and Court in Strasbourg concern the rights of organizations and companies. In Liberty's view only individual human beings can have human rights and any Bill of Rights should be restricted in its scope to give rights only to individuals.

Apart from the obvious issue of principle that human rights are for human beings there is a danger in allowing organizations and companies to use a Bill of Rights. The resources of such organizations are such that their rights will dominate any new system to the exclusion of the individuals that a Bill of Rights is intended to serve. In my view a Bill of Rights should protect those marginal groups of people who have no other way of influencing the political institutions in society and is not there to give a further right of redress to those who are already very powerful.

Organizations who have taken their cases to the institutions in Strasbourg have done so in a fairly restricted range of areas. First, they have claimed breaches of the right to property contained in Article 1 of the First Protocol. The issue of private property and the rights of the State is at the heart of political debate and the rights of organizations in such circumstances are not human rights.[41]

Secondly, trade unions and similar organizations have taken cases alleging violations of the right to freedom of assembly.[42] In my view the right of assembly is a right of the individual to join (or not to join) an assembly or organization and any violation of such rights can be dealt with by the individual taking up the case (albeit supported where necessary by a trade union).

Thirdly, newspapers have taken cases alleging violations of freedom of expression.[43] Although it must be admitted that this is a difficult issue I again would argue that the right belongs to the journalists not to the organization for which they work.

---

[41] The right to property is not for instance contained in the UN International Covenant on Civil and Political rights.

[42] E.g., *The Swedish Engine Drivers Union* (1976), Series A, vol. 20 or the closed shop case, *Young, James and Webster* v. *UK* (1981), Series A, vol. 44.

[43] E.g., the case of the *Sunday Times* campaign for the victims of the drug Thalidomide, *Sunday Times* v. *UK* (1979), Series A, vol. 30 or the publication of extracts of the book 'Spycatcher' in *Observer and Guardian Newspapers* v. *UK* (1991), Series A, vol. 216.

Organizations and companies would of course retain their right to petition the European Commission and Court of Human Rights regardless of the incorporation of the Convention into domestic law.

A Domestic Bill of Rights

Liberty has set out elsewhere the details of the Bill of Rights that it wishes to see implemented.[44] It is essential to this second stage to ensure that before any Bill of Rights is agreed that there is an adequate consultation process. A Bill of Rights, in order to be meaningful and to have a real effect and to be of real use needs to be known about and supported by the communities and peoples that it is designed to be used by. The support of lawyers and judges is not enough. In order to achieve such an aim this consultation process needs to be properly resourced and funded. Liberty has suggested that in order to carry out this task a Bill of Rights Commission should be established to consult and draft a Bill of Rights and that such a Commission would need at least two years to do this work.

I have discussed above some of the issues of content and the inadequacy of the European Convention as the text for a Bill of Rights above. I have also discussed some of the issues of remedies and who would have rights to take legal action in the context of the incorporation of the Convention and those brief thoughts also apply to any consideration of a domestic Bill of Rights.

Finally I would like to consider a few ideas on the issues of enforcement and entrenchment of a Bill of Rights. Liberty's proposals for enforcement try to retain an element of democratic control. The proposals involve dividing the rights in the Bill of Rights into two kinds. The basis remains that described above—the 'notwithstanding clause' model. However some rights in the Bill of Rights would be 'judicially entrenched' on the lines of the American Bill of Rights. A distinction between two kinds of rights can be found in the European Convention of Human Rights itself.[45] Liberty believes that courts (the High Court at least) should have the power to declare invalid other provisions of law incompatible with the terms of such articles and Parliament could not use the 'notwithstanding procedure' to overturn such decisions.[46]

[44] See n. 1 above.

[45] Art. 15 asserts that those Articles like the right to life, freedom from torture, freedom from slavery, the restriction on the creation of retrospective criminal offences, freedom of conscience, freedom from discrimination, and the right to democratic participation cannot be subject to derogation in times of war or other public emergencies whereas other articles can be.

[46] It may also be that other rights, such as some of the detailed provisions currently contained in Arts 5 and 6 of the European Convention, could also be included in this category.

The second category of rights would include all the remaining articles such as the right to privacy or freedom of expression, association or assembly. The rights in this second group are those which involve clear political conflict between different sets of rights. For instance, issues where the right to privacy clashes with the freedom of expression or information, or where the right to manifest one's beliefs conflicts with respect for, say, cultural diversity. In these cases it is suggested that where Acts of Parliament—rather than subsidiary legislation or administrative measures—are under review the final arbiter should not be the courts but should instead be Parliament, our elected representatives.

The second set of rights raise certain issues which are, at least for the foreseeable future, likely to remain problematic. To allow judges the ultimate say and not to allow Parliament any procedure whatsoever to overrule them on these issues would be a mistake.

Liberty has designed a new mechanism specifically to deal with this last category of rights.[47] A new committee of Parliament would be charged with the supervision of all human rights. We would want to see the committee selected so that it was not dominated by any one political party and particularly by the party which has formed the government. Liberty has also proposed that the committee would be assisted in its work by a new quango, a human rights commission, to monitor and promote human rights.

The committee would be given the task of considering new legislation and assessing its compliance with the Bill of Rights. Its role with regard to new laws would, however, be purely advisory. Its most crucial role would be initiated if primary legislation (or a part of it) had been struck down by the courts for infringing one of the rights contained in the second category. Here the committee could review the legislation and could have the power to certify that Parliament could subsequently re-enact the legislation without needing the 'notwithstanding clause' described above.

The advantage of this model is that it obviously allows for the introduction of a democratic element to have the final say in cases where there is a clash of rights. This not only avoids giving to the judiciary complete power to interpret the Bill of Rights but also allows democratic processes to have a role in shaping and developing fundamental rights.

Of course even Liberty's proposals will give the courts significantly more power to control the executive and other public bodies and to strike down primary legislation. For this reason Liberty believes that reform of the selection, appointment, and promotion of the judiciary to ensure fairness and equal opportunities must go hand in hand with these proposals.

---

[47] See Francesca Klug and John Wadham, 'A Peoples Charter: Liberty's Bill of Rights' and 'The Democratic Entrenchment of a Bill of Rights: Liberty's Proposals', *Public Law*, Winter 1993.

5

A Bill of Rights as Secular Ethics

FRANCESCA KLUG[1]

There are no rights in the United Kingdom.
There are too many rights in the United Kingdom and not enough responsibilities.

It is rare for a week to go by without both these propositions being aired by political commentators, politicians or academics. Indeed in the last couple of decades both perspectives have been argued with increasing vehemence.

Constitutional reformers and advocates of a Bill of Rights for the United Kingdom claim that in contrast to virtually every other democracy there are no rights in this country—however old and however revered—which the government of the day cannot take away at will. As illustrations, they point to such developments as the recent dilution of the historic right to remain silence under questioning and the abolition in 1983 of the ancient right of all children born on British soil to British citizenship. Even the right to jury trial—which stems from the Magna Carta of 1215—has been whittled away and is constantly under review. The following statement by Geoffrey Robertson QC typifies this concern:

rights and freedoms are in Britain at the mercy of Parliament which passes the statues which give them and take them away. And Parliament is controlled, with rare exceptions, by the executive government. . . . A democracy that subordinates fundamental rights to the exigencies of executive government leaves them dilapidated, outdated and legally insecure.[2]

Contrast that statement with the following. First, an opinion expressed by former lecturer and community activist Dick Atkinson for the think-tank Demos and second a statement by author and historian David Selbourne in his book *The Principle of Duty*:

[1] Francesca Klug is a fellow of Essex University's Human Right's Centre and a policy consultant on rights for Charter 88. She is the author of *A People's Charter*, Liberty's bill of rights.
[2] Geoffrey Robertson QC, *Freedom, the Individual and the Law* (Penguin, 1993), p. xiv.

The pendulum has swung so far from subjective authority and obligation towards reason authority and rights that their interdependence has been fractured and serious damage has been caused.[3]

the ethics and politics of dutiless right, demand-satisfaction and self-realisation through unimpeded freedom of action have been a costly moral failure in the corrupted liberal order.[4]

Are these different perceptions of the state of rights and liberties in the United Kingdom merely a reflection of the opposing political perspectives of their authors? Or is it possible that they are not mutually exclusive viewpoints? That they point to a complex reality only partially expressed by most political commentators? Could the absence of constitutionally protected rights described by Roberston actually contribute to the malaise depicted by Atkinson and Selbourne?

Wants or Rights?

To some extent the answer to this question lies in terminology. The term right is frequently used as if it were synonymous with freedom, license, want, or need. This pattern is as common amongst advocates of more and stronger rights as it is amongst their detractors. When the *Observer* columnist Melanie Phillips berates our 'rights-based society' for its 'destructive and exclusive failure' she points the finger at the government for its politics of 'vested interests' as much as at the left for 'treating rights as a religion'.[5] It is difficult to dispute her case that rights-speak is the vernacular of our age. Most groups or individuals with a demand or grievance invoke the ubiquitous term 'right' to legitimize their stand, much as the supernatural would have been summonsed in a previous era. Hence company directors claim to have a 'right' to be paid as much as the market can accommodate, smokers to smoke in public places, hunters to hunt and party-goers to party whenever and wherever they choose.

Whatever the merits or otherwise of these claims, their relationship with the fundamental rights enshrined in the European Convention on Human Rights and the various international human rights instruments spawned by the United Nations is tangential to say the least. They could be compared to the relationship between Shakespeare and Mills and Boon. They both stem from the same pedigree—English fiction—but the latter has been totally shorn of the depth and nuance which characterizes the former.

[3] Dick Atkinson, *The Common Sense of Community* (DEMOS, 1994), p. 53.
[4] David Selbourne, *The Principle of Duty* (Sinclair Stevenson, 1994), p. 277.
[5] The *Observer* 24 Oct. 1993.

Once this is understood the paradox whereby commentators like Phillips can casually refer to our 'culture of pre-eminent individual rights',[6] when the reality is that we have no fundamental rights in the United Kingdom, begins to make sense. Indeed it starts to become clear that these apparently opposing claims are not just a question of semantics. The absence of a domestic Bill of Rights—or even the incorporation within our law of the European Convention on Human Rights—means that there is anything but a culture of rights in the United Kingdom. There may to some degree be a culture of wants masquerading as rights but there is a woeful lack of understanding of the human rights philosophy that has evolved over the last fifty years. And in the context of that incomprehension it is hardly surprising if some commentators unwittingly collude with those they criticize and fail to make a distinction between rights and wants or rights and license.

The Communitarian Critique of Dutiless Rights

The assertion that we have too many rights and not enough duties in the United Kingdom has been given intellectual backing by a group of (mainly) American philosophers cum political activists known as communitarians. Beginning as a theoretical response to what was perceived as the individualistic theory of justice advanced by John Rawls and others in the 1970s,[7] the social movement known as communitarianism is described by its founder Amitai Etzioni, as 'aiming at shoring up the moral, social and political environment'.[8]

Etzioni, a professor at George Washington University and a former White House adviser to President Clinton, advocates a four-point agenda:

a moratorium on the minting of most, if not all, new rights; re-establishing the link between rights and responsibilities; recognising that some responsibilities do not entail rights and, most carefully, adjusting some rights to the changed circumstances.[9]

Etzioni is not an opponent of rights. Far from it. His argument is that rights are becoming devalued by the elevating of personal desires into the language of rights.

Once rights were very solomn moral/legal claims, ensconced in the constitution and treated with much reverence. We all lose if the publicity department of every special

---

[6] The *Observer* 19 Feb. 1996.

[7] John Rawls, *A Theory of Justice* (Cambridge Mass, 1977).

[8] Amitai Etzioni, *The Spirit of Community: rights, responsibilities and the communitarian agenda* (Crown, 1993), p. 247.

[9] *Ibid.*, p. 4.

interest can claim that someone's rights are violated every time they don't get what want.[10]

The 'core mission' for communitarians is to 'shore up morality' through the restoration of community—'we find reinforcement for our moral inclinations and provide reinforcement to our fellow human beings through the community'.[11]

Whilst this is not the place to delve into the details of communitarian philosophy, it is important to note that its influence in the UK is growing. When Etzioni visited Britain in March 1995 he was received by the leaders of the Labour and Liberal Democrat parties and cabinet ministers attended a dinner in his honour. Tickets for Etzioni's public lecture were sold out.[12] His ideas have been spread here by pamphleteers and columnists: most consistently by Geoff Mulgan and others associated with the think-tank Demos and by the journalist Melanie Phillips.[13] The principle ideas of communitarianism have also begun to creep into the literature on citizenship, particularly where active citizenship is advocated.[14]

Most notable is the growing influence of communitarian values on new Labour. Leading members of the party are increasingly emphasizing the importance of individual citizens fulfilling their duties and responsibilities if the project of a revitalized society is to be achieved. In a lecture to a local community group in November 1995 Shadow Home Secretary, Jack Straw, asserted that if Britain is to become a society based on mutual responsibility:

the most important change involves a change in attitude. We need to break out of the language of dutiless rights and begin insisting upon mutual responsibility. Rights and duty go hand in hand.[15]

In their book *The Blair Revolution* Peter Mandelson MP and Roger Liddle argue that this emphasis on responsibilities is one of the defining features of New Labour. 'Whereas the left appeared to argue for rights without responsibilities and that one was responsible for oneself alone, New Labour stresses the importance of mutual obligations'.[16]

This claim is reflected in the new Clause Four of Labour's constitution—which defines the party's aims and values—with the statement that 'the

[10] Amitai Etzioni, p. 6.   [11] *Ibid.*, pp. 30–1.

[12] 'Down with rights' The *Economist*, 18 Mar. 1995.

[13] 'Import Duties' Paul Anderson and Kevin Davey, *New Statesman and Society*, 3 March 1995.

[14] E.g., see David Prior *et al*, *Citizenship, Rights, Community and Participation* (Pitman, 1995).

[15] Speech to Community Links, 7 Nov. 1995.

[16] Peter Mandelson and Roger Liddle, *The Blair Revolution: can New Labour deliver?* (Faber & Faber, 1996).

rights we enjoy reflect the duties we owe' (and not, it should be noted, the other way round).

There can be little doubt that this emphasis on duties and responsibilities reflects a growing sense of unease about a society which appears to be increasingly fragmented. For many on the centre left this is blamed on the corrosive effect of the entry of market forces into virtually all areas of social as well as economic life with its emphasis on competition and individual achievement and its creation of winners and losers. For the centre right and an expanding section of the left it is the decline of the two-parent family which is the cause of this disintegration witnessed by the soaring divorce rate and an apparent explosion of juvenile crime (although there is some debate about whether this is largely due to a small number of youths committing an increasing number of crimes). Others blame the waning of religion and what is perceived to be an absence of moral values taught in schools.

The problem, however, in importing Etzioni's ideas lock, stock, and barrel is that they have developed in response to factors which are by no means identical to those which prevail in the United Kingdom. When he calls for a halt on creating new rights he is writing in the context of a society which has the oldest set of constitutionally entrenched rights in the world. When he laments that the only responsibility that is assumed in the American 'rights dialect' is to avoid harming others he is referring to the philosophy of the American Constitution. Although related, this is significantly different to the international human rights standards which developed since the Second World War and which the American Government has only begun to ratify since President Clinton came into office. It is these latter standards which would form the basis of any Bill of Rights for the United Kingdom.

The American Model for Entrenching Rights

To fully understand this difference it is necessary to become acquainted with the basic values of the American Bill of Rights and the degree to which subsequent international human rights developments represented a departure from them. This is especially necessary because of the common assumption in this—as in many other areas—that the American model is the gold standard which all others necessarily follow.

Whilst there are substantial differences between them, the 1791 American Bill of Rights and the 1789 French Declaration of the Rights of Man both represent what could be called the first age of human rights. Two characteristics of this period, commonly known as the Enlightenment, are reflected in these Bills of Rights. First, was the widespread (although not uncontested) belief in 'natural rights'. This stemmed from the seventeenth century English philosopher John Locke who regarded certain fundamental rights as pertaining to the pre-social state of nature to which all of human-kind could be said to belong. Second, was the common struggle for democracy and human rights waged against autocratic rulers who sought legitimacy for their rule in the divine rather than the terrestrial world of 'natural rights'.

Strongly influenced by these factors, the founding fathers of the American Constitution held that all human beings are the carriers of certain inalienable rights. Notwithstanding the representative and federal democracy created by the Constitution, majoritarianism was to have its limits. These limits were set down by the broad values expressed in (what was originally) ten amendments to the Constitution, otherwise known as the American Bill of Rights.[17] This 'higher law'—to which all subsequent policy and legislation would be subject—was the mechanism by which the government, representing the will of the majority, would be prevented from trampling on the rights of individuals.

The eminent professor of jurisprudence Ronald Dworkin urges a 'moral reading' of the American Bill of Rights which, he argues, commits the United States to the following political and legal ideas:

government must treat all those subject to its dominion as having equal moral and political status; it must attempt, in good faith, to treat them all with concern; and it must respect whatever individual freedoms are indispensable to those ends. . . .[18]

Whilst there is undoubtedly an ethical vision which drives the American Bill of Rights, the principal duty than can be inferred from its terms is a negative one: to refrain from disturbing the rights of others.[19] Duties as correlative of rights—your duty not to invade my privacy may be justified by my right to privacy—is one of the hallmarks of fundamental rights.[20] Yet it is reasonable to claim that under the American model there is no wider vision of the common good or community beyond than that of discreet individuals enabled by the Bill of Rights to pursue life, liberty, and happiness.

[17] Another limit to this democracy was of course that it did not include women or slaves; the latter being relegated to 'three fifths of all other persons' in the original constitution Art. 1, s. 2.

[18] 'The Moral Reading of the Constitution', Ronald Dworkin, The *New York Review of Books*, 1 Mar. 1996. See also R. Dworkin *Freedom's Law* (Oxford University Press, 1996).

[19] See 'From natural law to the rights of man: a European perspective on American debates', Knud Haakonssen, in *A Culture of Rights, the Bill of Rights in philosophy, politics and law 1791 and 1991*, M. Lacey and K. Haakonssen (eds) (Cambridge University Press, 1991).

[20] Ronald Dworkin, *Taking Rights Seriously* (Duckworth, 1977).

International Human Rights Standards

The phrase 'human rights' did not come into common parlance until after the second world war. From the horrors of the Holocaust grew a fresh resolve to create a code of ethics which would unite the entire international community. The mass annihilation of Jews and other minority communities brought home the need for mechanisms other than those based entirely on majority rule. No longer was the doctrine of national sovereignty—under which States had no authority to interfere in each other's internal affairs—to be used to justify appeasement of a brutal or tyrannical regime.

Sterile debates about whether 'natural rights' existed or not were abandoned in favour of drafting international treaties which were binding on the States which had ratified them and which would be enforced by international or regional bodies. If human rights were protected by international law—and States voluntarily subscribed to this law—then the dispute which began in the Enlightenment over whether fundamental rights could be said to exist outside the law, was perceived to be largely irrelevant.

The United Nations Universal Declaration on Human Rights (UDHR), adopted in 1948 in the immediate aftermath of the war, set down the standards which became the basis for all subsequent international and regional human rights instruments. Classical rights and liberties like freedom of speech, assembly, association, and movement, along with 'second generation' social and economic rights and rights to equal treatment and democratic participation were established as fundamental principles which the whole international community should aspire to. The twin International Covenants on Civil and Political and Economic, Social and Cultural rights (ICCPR and ICESCR respectively) which were adopted in 1966, were designed to turn the broad principles in the UDHR into binding obligations on States. Together with the Universal Declaration they comprise what became known as the International Bill of Human Rights.

Meanwhile member States of the Council of Europe (another post-war institution) adopted the European Convention on Human Rights (ECHR) which came into force in 1953. The European Social Charter, the complementary document to the ECHR, was adopted in 1961. The Organisation of American States adopted the American Declaration of the Rights and Duties of Man in 1948. This was succeeded by the American Convention on Human Rights (AMCHR) which came into force in 1978. The African Charter on Human and Peoples' Rights was adopted by the Organisation of African Unity in 1981. Together with numerous single issue human rights covenants and conventions on race, women, children, torture, and so forth these instruments reflect an explosion in the development of human rights thinking over the last fifty years.

Whilst they differ from each other in significant ways, regional and international human rights instruments have at least three common features which bind them and which set them apart from the original American and French Bills of Rights. First, they are universal in their application. With the exception of a few specified articles they apply to everyone within the jurisdiction of the states which have ratified them, regardless of citizenship or other status. It should be noted that their other claim to universality—that they represent values which are common to all cultures—is increasingly contested.[21]

Second, they are enforced or supervised by regional or international bodies to which States can make complaints against each other in defiance of the doctrine of national sovereignty. (Provided that their governments have ratified the relevant articles, individuals can also complain about violations by their own states to the Human Rights Committee which supervises the ICCPR and the European and Inter-American Commissions which provide the first stage in the enforcement mechanism of the ECHR and AMCHR respectively).

Third, the broad human rights standards enshrined in these instruments are to varying degrees qualified and limitations are placed on their application.

Fourth, they lay down legal obligations for States, and moral responsibilities for individuals, which go beyond simply refraining from interfering with the rights of others.

It is these last two features which are of particular relevance when considering the ethical basis of any Bill of Rights based on international standards. It is therefore worth examining them in greater detail to consider whether the absence of any constitutional rights in the United Kingdom has contributed to the sense of moral erosion which preoccupies so many commentators.[22]

Are Duties Inherent in International Human Rights Standards?

It is clear that individuals do have duties under international law. This was explicitly stated at the Nuremberg Tribunal set up to try Nazi war criminals after the Second World War. On 1 October 1946 the Tribunal delivered the following judgment:

---

[21] See, e.g., Henry Steiner and Philip Alston, *International Human Rights in Context: law, politics, morals* (Clarendon, 1996), Ch. 4.

[22] There are many texts which describe international human rights instruments and their enforcement mechanisms but none are more comprehensive and easier to use than Paul Sieghart, *International Law of Human Rights* (Clarendon, 1983).

international law imposes duties and liabilities upon individuals as well as upon states. . . . crimes against international law are committed by men, not by abstract entities and only by punishing individuals who commit such crimes can the provisions of international law be enforced[23]

That individual responsibility is inherent in international human rights philosophy is underlined in the preamble to the Universal Declaration of Human Rights.

The General Assembly proclaims this Universal Declaration of Human rights as a common standard of achievement for all peoples of all nations, to the end that *every individual* and every organ of society, keeping this Declaration constantly in mind, shall strive by teaching and education to promote respect for these right and freedoms and by progressive measures, national and international, to secure their universal recognition and observance (emphasis added).

In addition, Article 29, clause 1, explicitly declares the duties or responsibilities each individual has to their community, 'Everyone has duties to the community in which alone the free and full development of his [*sic*] personality is possible'. That this involves a positive commitment to upholding human rights, rather than merely refraining from damaging the rights of others, is evident by the fact that the latter obligation is covered in the second clause in the Article. This refers to 'securing due recognition and respect of the rights and freedoms of others' as one of the grounds for limiting the exercise of rights and freedoms along with 'meeting the just requirements of morality, public order and the general welfare in a democratic society'.

It is not possible to find, as the American communitarian author Mary Ann Glendon laments, 'in the familiar language of [the American] Declaration of Independence or Bill of Rights anything comparable to [these] statements in the Universal Declaration of Human Rights'.[24]

An examination of the papers which record the debates leading up the final draft of the International Covenant on Civil and Political Rights (the *travaux préparatoires*), suggests that it was the intention of the drafters that individuals be obliged to respect the human rights they contain.[25] The preamble to both the ICCPR, and its twin Covenant the ICESCR, stipulates that:

the individual, having duties to other individuals and to the community to which he [sic] belongs, is under a responsibility to strive for the promotion and observance of the rights recognised in the present Covenant.

---

[23] Transcript of Proceedings (1 Oct. 1946), quoted in Andrew Clapham, *Human Rights in the Private Sphere* (Clarendon, 1993), p. 96.

[24] Quoted in Etzioni, see above n. 7, p. 39.

[25] Quoted in Clapham, see above n. 22, p. 97.

The Inter-American Declaration of the Rights and Duties of Man, which was actually adopted a few months before the Universal Declaration of Human Rights, contains a catalogue of duties in ten separate Articles. What distinguishes these from the UDHR and ICCPR is that they are not integrated into the rights that the ADHR upholds but are a discreet list of obligations. These include duties to work, serve in the armed forces when required, and obey the law and 'other legitimate commands of the authorities'.

Interestingly, these duties to not appear in the ADHR's successor instrument, the American Convention on Human Rights, which is the legally binding document. Instead there is a short chapter headed 'Personal Responsibilities' which stipulates the responsibility of every person to their 'family, community and mankind' and which defines the grounds on which rights can be limited, including the 'just demands of the general welfare'.

The only other international instrument with a separate section on duties is the African Charter on Human and People's Rights. The individual is required under Article 29 to uphold a series of duties. These involve, amongst others, preserving 'the harmonious development of the family', 'respect [for] his [*sic*] parents at all times', and 'the promotion and achievement of African unity' and 'positive African cultural values'. Like the American Declaration of Rights, this is largely a declaratory instrument. The African Commission on Human and People's Rights, which is charged with applying its provisions, has no associated court to enforce it.

It is evident, then, that no international human rights treaty seeks to provide *individuals* with *legally binding* duties which are not bound up with the requirement to uphold the rights of others. To do so would, as some of the examples from the American Declaration and African Charter suggest, involve imposing a degree of coercion that negates many of the principles, like freedom of conscience and privacy, that international human rights standards seek to uphold. It would be reminiscent of the practices of most former Communist regimes where the apparent right to work meant the duty to work and constitutional rights became discredited as duties disguised as rights.

There is nevertheless running through international human rights standards a vision of community and of responsible individuals which to some degree overlaps with the one Etzioni describes. To take the European Convention as an example, there is throughout a reference to the need to balance a given right against a string of other considerations. These include the interests of national security or public safety, the prevention of disorder or crime and the protection of health, morals, and the rights and freedoms of others.

The moral reading of the Convention is unmistakable. Whilst there are certain fundamental rights which adhere to all individuals because of their humanity, these do not apply in a vacuum but have to be balanced against the rights of other individuals and the needs of society as a whole.

There is, for example, no equivalent to the first amendment of the American Constitution which stipulates that 'Congress shall make no law' which infringes free speech. On the contrary, Article 10 of the ECHR explicitly states that the exercise of free expression 'carries with it duties and responsibilities' (the only explicit references to these terms in the Convention). The ICCPR goes even further. Not only is there the same reference to duties and responsibilities in Article 19 on free speech, but Article 20 prohibits incitement to national, racial, or religious hatred; a clear example how the rights of the individual are balanced against the needs of the community above and beyond the requirement of correlative duties. In other words, it is not just that you must allow others the free speech that you are entitled to yourself, you must temper this with the obligation not to incite racial hatred.

This approach is summarized in draft guidelines produced by the UN's Commission on Human Rights in 1985 on the *Right and Responsibility of Individuals to Promote and Protect Human Rights.*

Responsibility, like human rights, shall be considered indivisible. In a responsible society human rights will have a positive and creative social thrust. Accordingly, every individual, group and organ of society have a responsibility to strive by teaching and education to promote the achievement of a social and international order in which the rights and freedom set forth in the Universal Declaration of Human Rights and the International Covenants on Human Rights, and other international instruments on human rights, can be fully realised.[26]

In specific terms it is clear that although the binding international human rights treaties have a good deal less to say about duties than rights, the concept of responsibility is woven throughout the texts. States have an explicit responsibility in both the European Convention (Article 1) and International Covenant on Civil and Political Rights (Article 2) to secure the rights and freedoms they uphold. The jurisprudence developed by the UN's Human Rights Committe, and the European Court of Human Rights, has established that this does not just require the State to refrain from violating individuals' rights as is classically expressed in the American model. It involves the State taking positive action.

This primarily means the State making certain that its own organs comply with the treaties' terms—as in securing the right to a fair trial or adequate detention and prison conditions. But it also entails passing legislation and providing regulations which ensure that no one with the power to do so

---

[26] Principle 19, Draft Body of Principles and Guidelines on the Right and Responsibility of Individuals, Groups and Organs of Society to Promote and Protect Human Rights and Fundamental Freedoms, United Nations Commission on Human Rights, E/CN.4/ Sub.2/1985/30, 25 June 1985.

violates the rights of other. This responsibility is sometimes referred to by the German term *Drittwirkung der Grundrechte*—literally third party effect of fundamental rights (although there is no mechanism by which individuals can bring direct claims against private individuals under the European Convention or International Covenants).

As the European Convention has evolved over time it has become increasingly apparent that States are under a positive obligations to protect individuals against infringements of their rights by private people or bodies, although the full extent of this has yet to be tested.[27] Cases where this responsibility has been established include the need for protection against threats by an employer of dismissal for union activity or not joining a specific union;[28] the requirement to take reasonable measures to protect peaceful demonstrators from disruption by other individuals[29] and the obligation to adopt 'measures designed to secure respect for private life even in the sphere of the relations of individuals themselves'.[30]

The Human Rights Committee has issued a number of General Comments which indicate the extent to which individuals should be held responsible by the state for breaches of the Covenant. For example, to comply with Article 7—which prohibits torture or cruel, inhuman or degrading treatment or punishment—states are required to indicate which provisions of their criminal law prohibit these practices, whether they are carried out by public officials or 'private persons'.[31] Similarly, under Article 24 on the rights of children the state is required to intervene where parents and the family 'seriously fail in their duties, ill treat or neglect the child'.[32]

The UN's Conventions on race and gender are likewise replete with references to the State's obligation to eliminate discrimination in the private sphere. Article 2(d) of the International Convention on the Elimination of all Forms of Racial Discrimination, for example, requires each State to prohibit 'racial discrimination by any persons, group or organisation'.

A Bill of Rights and Responsibilities for the United Kingdom?

From this necessarily brief review of the role of responsibilities and duties in international human rights law a picture of the potential impact of a British Bill of Rights should begin to emerge.

---

[27] See D. J. Harris *et al*, *Law of the European Convention on Human Rights* (Butterworths, 1995), p. 21.

[28] *James, Young and Webster* v. *UK*, A 44 para. 49 (1981).

[29] *Plattform 'Arzte fur das Leben* v. *Austria*, A.139 para. 32 (1988).

[30] *X and Y* v. *Netherlands*, A 91 para. 23 (1985).

[31] General Comment no. 20(44) Art. 7, CCPR/C/21/Rev.1/Add.3.

[32] General Comment A/44/40.

If the European Convention were incorporated into United Kingdom law, as both the Labour and Liberal Democrat parties have pledged, then the primary effect would be to provide international human rights standards with a constitutional protection they have never before received in the United Kingdom. According to most proposals under consideration, the rights and freedoms in the ECHR would amount to a 'higher law' which legislation and the policy and procedures of government and public officials would be bound by.[33]

In this sense we would, for the first time, have fundamental rights in the United Kingdom; political parties could no longer simply barter our rights away in an unseemly Dutch auction whenever elections are drawing near. Whether it be the shackling of women political prisoners at hospital visits, executive control over the release dates of life prisoners, legislation which criminalizes many kinds of peaceful protest, or the sacking of gay and lesbian armed service personnel on the grounds of their sexuality, these decisions or policies would be subject to a clear and written code. Rather than political expediency or populist outcry (usually mediated through the tabloid press rather than any serious test of public opinion) a set of fundamental values, based on a clear moral philosophy, would be the driving force behind such policies.

To argue that this would usher in a further deluge of dutiless rights when what we need is more responsibilities is to miss the point entirely. By incorporating international human rights standards into our law we would simultaneously create a new set of responsibilities, some of which would take the form of legal requirements, others moral exhortations. Rights would be balanced not only against each other but against specific limitations which apply to most of the Articles in the Convention. Indeed many would argue that far from reinforcing liberty at all costs the limitations placed on rights under the Convention, such as the protection of national security or morals, are too numerous and too loosely drawn. Others, like the legitimate taking of life where action is 'lawfully taken for the purpose of quelling a riot' (Article 2.2(c)) or the lawful detention of 'alcoholics' or 'vagrants', whether or not they have committed a crime (Article 5.1(e)), are arguably more to do with the concerns of the British government lawyers who drafted the Convention at the end of the 1940s than the international human rights standards laid down in the Universal Declaration on Human Rights.

---

[33] Although there is some dispute about whether Parliament would ever agree to entrench a Bill of Rights in the manner of the American model, most commentators predict that future legislation would be required to comply with its terms unless it *expressly* stated otherwise. For proposals for 'democratic entrenchment' see *A People's Charter*, Liberty's Bill of Rights (1991).

The first layer of responsibilities would belong to the State which, as we have seen, would have to ensure that its legislation and policies, and the actions of its officials, do not only not violate the Convention but are positively engaged in complying with its terms. As a minimum this would involve reviewing all past and present laws, policies, and procedures (to comply with Article 1) and could be extended to include such measure as widely publicizing the terms of the Convention and requiring it to be taught in schools.

Incorporation would make the conduct of government, in particular, more accountable. The substantive values in the European Convention, and the manner in which they are applied by the European Court of Human Rights, would form an open part of the judicial review process (instead of judges quarrelling over whether they can apply them, as at present, and in most cases failing to do so).[34] No longer would the situation prevail where a decision must be outrageous in its defiance of logic before it can be overturned by the courts, but if it is outrageous in its defiance of human rights the courts are largely powerless to intervene.

Just as significant, incorporation of the European Convention should result in a change in the moral climate in which governments currently operate. Helena Kennedy QC, delivering the Stevenson Lecture on Citizenship in February 1996, described the present moral vacuum the government operates in:

We have seen anti-discriminatory initiatives derided by Government as politically correct and equality of opportunity insidiously pushed off the agenda as an issue of national concern . . . Tolerance is now being presented by some public and media figures as only a good thing in small doses, particularly when it comes to refugees. Yet all our historic experience tells us that a just and peaceful society is only possible where there is tolerance and respect for diversity.

It may even not be too naive to suppose that with a Bill of Rights we would be spared the unedifying spectacle of MPs debating whether political embarrassment is, or is not, a reasonable cause for (knowingly or unknowingly) misleading parliament, as happened in the aftermath of the *Scott Report*. The assumption would be in favour of releasing information on the grounds that it is a fundamental human right to receive and impart information under the European Convention. This right can only be limited under specified circumstances such as to protect national security or public safety—and then only when 'necessary in a democratic society'—but never to save ministers' skins.

---

[34] The influence of the ECHR on court judgements and the extent to which the doctrine of proprtionality is applied by domestic courts was the subject of research for F. Klug, K. Starmer & S. Weir, *The Three Pillars of Liberty, the Democratic Audit of the UK* (Routledge, forthcoming).

Much of the commentary and correspondence about *Scott* in the national press pointed to the hypocrisy of ministers lamenting the apparent disintegration of moral values in the rest of society when time and again they demonstrate a lack of ethical behaviour in their own decisions and actions. Stewart Steven, for example, writing in the *Mail on Sunday* in the wake of *Scott* declared:

This is why I, for one, am mightily relieved that this country is a signatory to the European Convention on Human Rights which allows a British subject . . . to believe that in the final analysis—whatever a supine Parliament might allow, however a malign Government might ordain—values enshrined in some universal notion of what is acceptable and what is not can be applied to him [*sic*].[35]

A Bill of Rights based on the European Convention could also involve creating a new responsibility for local authorities to comply with its terms; much as they are required to promote good race relations under section 71 of the Race Relations Act. Council committees would be obliged to examine current practice—from child protection to planning applications—for compliance with the substantive or procedural requirements of the Convention. Such action has already been taken by some selected authorities in relation to their obligations under the 1989 UN Convention on the Rights of the Child.

The second layer of responsibility would apply to any individuals or corporate bodies which perform a public function. The courts have already determined that where there is a 'public element' decisions are subject to judicial review (unless the applicant's relationship with the body or individual is purely consensual).[36] As with the executive, the difference from now would be that judicial review would be subject to the Convention.

Given the underdeveloped nature of the public/private law divide in the United Kingdom the door is open for the application of the Convention in the private sector. There is, in theory, nothing to stop the legislation which incorporates the Convention from extending this second layer of responsibility to anyone or any association with the power to inflict human rights violations on others. In his path-breaking book, *Human Rights in the Private Sphere*, Andrew Clapham makes a number of proposals in this vein. He suggests that judicial bodies dealing with allegations of human rights violations should discard the public/private distinction and '*examine the harm to the victim*'[37] (his emphasis). Only then should they decide whether the harm in question is covered by the Convention.

[35] *Mail on Sunday*, 25 Feb. 1996. Other examples include 'A walk-on role for morality', Frances Wheen, *Guardian*, 21 Feb. 1996; 'Why we view our politicians with such contempt,' Simon Barrington-Ward, *Daily Express*, 26 Feb. 1996 and 'Scott and morality', leader comment, The *Scotsman*, 26 Feb. 1996.

[36] *R.* v. *Panel on Takeovers and Mergers*, ex p. *Datafin plc* [1987] QB 815.

[37] Clapham, above n. 23, p. 352 and Ch. 5.

He also suggests that if the 1990 New Zealand Bill of Rights model was adopted—which explicitly states that the acts of the judiciary are covered by its terms—then where disputes by private actors are determined in court they would seemingly be covered by the rights in the Convention. Under this model the incorporated Convention could not be used directly in legal disputes between individuals or private bodies but could be applied where a civil case is already before a judge, 'In this way human rights principles become relevant for the determination of conflicts in the private sphere'.[38]

An alternative approach was proposed by the late Labour MP, Sam Silkin, in his 1971 *Protection of Human Rights Bill*. He suggested establishing a 'national tribunal of Human rights' where violations 'by public authority or by private organisation' could be reviewed.[39]

These proposals would address the concern that legal duties imposed by the Convention only apply to public bodies or functions; a matter of increasing relevance as the private sector in the United Kingdom takes on more and more responsibility for areas affecting fundamental rights. With private prisons, private security firms confronting protesters, private companies holding vast amounts of personal information on computer, and private shops and shopping malls making widespread use of video surveillance the responsibilities of some private corporations mirror that of the public sphere. Nevertheless there are limits to this cross-over. In many instances, private bodies do not have the same duties as the state. A religious group, for example, must be entitled to exclude members of another faith, and a political party to exclude members of a different belief.

The right to privacy enshrined in the Convention would itself would set limits to the extent to which legally enforceable duties would apply to private individuals. Clapham's 'victim' concept is a useful way to prevent the abuse of power in the domestic sphere from necessarily being deemed outside the scope of protection of human rights law (although perhaps an alternative term could be found). At the same time many aspects of private relationships must, if the right to privacy is to mean anything, remain outside the scope of legally enforceable Convention rights. Decisions about fertility and voluntary sexual practices provide two examples. Grey areas which do not fit neatly into either side are bound to remain; the thorny issue of the right of parents to bring up their children according to their own religious or moral philosophy versus freedom of conscience and gender equality for girls is one such issue.

There is an argument for saying that questions like this should anyway not be resolved through legally enforceable rights. Instead they belong to the third layer of responsibilities; that which pertains to each individual not as a result of judicial enforcement, but as a result of the moral values

---

[38] Clapham, above n. 23, pp. 339–42.   [39] H. C. Hansard, 2 April 1971. Col. 1854.

imparted through a Bill of Rights. And here it must be acknowledged that a Bill based on a wider set of standards than the European Convention is likely to have a significantly greater impact.

Such a Bill could include the right of children to 'special safeguards and care' and the family to 'the necessary protection and assistance' laid down in the UN Convention on the Rights of the Child. It could incorporate the 1951 Geneva Convention on the status of refugees in United Kingdom law. It could cover prisoners' rights by including the UN's Standard Minimum Rules for the Treatment of Prisoners. It could provide a clearer right to freedom of information as provided by Article 19 of the International Covenant on Civil and Political Rights. And it could introduce a general right not to be discriminated against in any sphere of the law as enshrined in Article 26 of the Covenant, rather than the more limited protection afforded by Article 14 of the European Convention. (So limited in fact that the Human Rights Unit in the Foreign and Commonwealth Office recognizes that it would not provide adequate protection for minority rights in the context of a future settlement for Northern Ireland).

Such a Bill of Rights, based on a broad spectrum of international human rights standards, could provide a set of moral values to guide the whole of society, children and adults alike. The Government's chief curriculum adviser, Dr. Nicholas Tate, laments the lack of ethical teaching in schools and proposes a national agreement on the values that schools should be promoting.[40] A Bill of Rights which encompasses a broad range of international human rights standards could provide precisely that.

The attempt by this government to proffer specifically Christian values as the basis of moral teaching simply will not work in a society where most children are not brought up in religious households and many who are belong to other religions. International human rights standards provide a set of secular ethics which, whilst drawing upon the moral teachings of all the major religions, attempt to express universal and timeless values. As we have seen, this claim to universality is challenged, in particular by many of Muslim faith. However it remains the case that most countries in the world have ratified the main UN instruments. This may not have changed their practices in many cases but it does suggest that there already exists a set of unifying ethics which it should be beholden on schools to teach.

The possibility that a Bill of Rights could achieve this kind of influence on peoples' moral choices and decisions must be linked to the involvement individuals and groups have in its adoption. It is often argued that a Bill of Rights based on the Convention is the only one this society could tolerate. The Government is already required to comply with its terms by the European Court of Human Rights; would not it be better if our own courts,

[40] *Times Educational Supplement*, 19 Jan. 1996.

rather than a foreign one, were set this task?. At least the Convention can attract all—party support; a Bill of Rights which is broader in scope is bound to lead to dispute and debate.

The reason why there is validity in this argument is the very reason why an incorporated Convention on its own is unlikely to bring about the kind of general moral revitalization that many believe our fragmented society needs. Precisely because the Convention is already drafted and already attracts consensus there would be little to consult upon. If Canada (prior to the adoption of the Charter of Rights and Freedoms in 1982), and now South Africa, can spend years consulting on the contents and means of enforcement of a Bill of Rights why can't the United Kingdom?

The South African Constitutional Assembly has even produced a journal, *Constitutional Talk*, complete with cartoons, pictures, and explanations of the implications of various options. Readers are invited to respond to suggested alternatives for inclusion in the final Bill of Rights (an interim one is now in force). The Assembly has received over a million individual submissions on the contents of a Bill of Rights and they are still coming in. Among other issues, they are consulting upon the question of *Drittwirkung* and whether internationally recognized social and economic rights should be part of their bill. It is also possible to imagine victims' rights forming part of any such consultation process in the United Kingdom.

It is presumably because other countries' experiences suggest that such an exercise has the potential to unite rather than divide—even if there are disputes and debates along the way—that the Labour party has expressed its commitment to following up incorporation of the European Convention with a domestic Bill of Rights. Jack Straw has described this as 'our great project to give the British people the rights and responsibilities upon which a properly functioning civil society is founded'.[41]

Conclusion

The success of any future Bill of Rights should not be measured in terms of how many legal cases it generates. As with the race relations and sex discrimination legislation of the 1970s, it should influence the moral values of society as a whole; not merely regulate the actions of the State. If it were truly successful there should in fact be far fewer civil rights cases than currently. In this sense the goals which drive the demand for a Bill of Rights for the United Kingdom are consistent with the communitarian vision discussed earlier. Both assume that as far as civil society is concerned, widely shared values which involve an intricate balance between rights and

---

[41] Speech to Labour Party Conference, 5 Oct. 1995.

responsibilities can be morally persuasive in themselves, without necessarily resorting to law.

Much of what Communitarians favour has little to do with laws and regulations which ultimately draw on the coercive powers of the state . . . Does that mean that every act of moral observance is completely and purely voluntary? The answer is yes, if by 'voluntary' acts we mean those propelled by moral voices within the community that are neither forced not motivated by the threat of a lawsuit or a gun.[42]

Furthermore, Etzioni recognizes that communities can be sites of oppression as well as sources of moral cohesion; that in the name of strongly-held moral beliefs minorities of all kinds can, and have been, persecuted by majoritarian communities. His resolution for 'keeping moral voices within bounds?'—

the bill of rights, which singles out matters that are exempt from majority rule and from typical democratic rule making and in which minority and individual rights take precedence.[43]

Or as Amy Gutman wrote in her contribution to a reader on *Communitarianism and Individualism*, 'The enforcement of liberal rights, not the absence of settled community, stands between the Moral Majority and the contemporary equivalent of witch-hunting'.[44]

In this context Etzioni's proposed moratorium on minting new rights to swing the pendulum in favour of responsibilities makes no sense in a society without any constitutional rights. It is hard to imagine that he would be opposed to a Bill of Rights for the United Kingdom.

Yet there are significant ways in which the communitarian project parts company from the international human rights approach to moral values. Where the latter provides broad brush principles the former offers detailed prescriptions, from shoring up the nuclear family to the way schools should be run. Where international human rights philosophy supposes that shared principles and values can themselves create a common identity and a sense of the common good, communitarianism is wedded to specific institutional solutions. Where international human rights standards encourage, but do not require, individuals to participate in public life, communitarianism puts a high value on active citizenship.

Perhaps the most significant difference is that whilst communitarians advocate duties that are not connected to rights, international human rights philosophy views the two as delicately balanced. This latter vision offers a set of secular ethics where the dignity of human beings is not sacrificed in

---

[42] Etzioni, above n. 8, p. 39.   [43] *Ibid.*, p. 53 and p. 50.
[44] 'Communitarian Critics of Liberalism' Amy Gutman, in *Communitarianism and Individualism*, S. Avineri and A. de-Shalit (eds) (OUP, 1992).

the name of the common good. Written into all the major international human rights instruments is an attempt to reconcile the rights of individuals with the needs of the community as a whole.

If this century of failed utopias has taught us anything is it not where philosophies which place duties above rights can *ultimately* lead? From where do they receive legitimacy? Almost always from religious or political ideologies—belief systems which are born from idealism and moral values but which, once they are promoted to State ideologies, die from the reaction against the tyranny they have unleashed. Tyranny against those who are socially excluded because they have a different (or no) religion or belief system or because their culture or lifestyle simply does not fit. It was precisely these circumstances which provided the inspiration for the belief in fundamental human rights in the first place.

It was the Holocaust and the gulag, in particular, that produced the motor for the explosion in human rights standards over the last fifty years. Standards which offer *all* belief systems State protection provided they do not incite racial hatred or cause harm to others. Standards where entitlement to civil rights is not dependent on performing duties. This is an important point which clearly distinguishes human rights philosophy from many belief systems which value duties unconnected to rights. Individuals may lose rights only to the extent that is absolutely necessary to protect others. As the European Convention stipulates, whilst it is legitimate to deprive individuals of their liberty for committing a crime, they do not consequently lose their right to life, to a fair trial, to free speech or to privacy.

A glimpse from a book titled *Duties of Women* by Frances Power, published in 1881, illustrates the limits of a moral philosophy based only on duties—in this instance Christian duties—*even when shorn of the power of a totalitarian regime.*

I believe it is the high duty of women to discountenance by driving out of society those who are guilty of . . . offences either against the great laws of Chastity or of Honesty . . . and I maintain that it is the duty of every woman to refuse to associate with persons who are notoriously guilty of them. . . . I insist that they are no longer fit to join in social pleasures . . . and that no woman ought to receive them in her own house . . .[45]

Such sentiments may have resonance in one age but are likely to seem absurd even to a younger generation of the same era. It is not difficult to see why such prescriptions have not stood the test of time and sound quaint and old-fashioned. Tom Paine, by contrast, who wrote *Rights of Man* almost a century earlier, still speaks to the modern age when he dealt with the question of the relationship between rights and duties.

---

[45] Frances Power, *Duties of Women* (Williams & Norgate, 1881), p. 131.

When the [French] Declaration of Rights was before the National Assembly, some of its members remarked, that if a Declaration of Rights was published, it should be accompanied by a Declaration of Duties. The observation discovered a mind that reflected and it only erred by not reflecting far enough. A Declaration of Rights is, by reciprocity, a Declaration of Duties also. *Whatever is my right as a man, is also the right of another; and it becomes my duty to guarantee as well as to possess.* (emphasis added)[46]

Cynics will no doubt declare that human rights philosophy is yet another failed utopia which has never lived up to the aspirations of Paine and all who have followed him. The fact that terrible human rights abuses are committed by regimes which have subscribed to international human rights standards is beyond doubt. But this is surely evidence of the weakness of human rights enforcement mechanisms; it is not a failure of the standards themselves or the philosophy which lies behind them.

[46] Thomas Paine, *Rights of Man* ([1791], Penguin 1984), p. 114.

6

Does Britain Need a Bill of Rights?

RONALD DWORKIN[1]

The Culture of Liberty

Great Britain was once a fortress for freedom. It claimed the great philosophers of liberty—Milton and Locke and Paine and Mill. Its legal tradition is irradiated with liberal ideas: that people accused of crime are presumed to be innocent, that no one owns another's conscience, that a man's home is his castle, that speech is the first liberty because it is central to all the rest. But now Britain offers much less formal legal protection to central freedoms than most democracies do, including most of Britain's neighbours in Europe. These democracies have written constitutions that guarantee individual freedom, and their judges are charged with ensuring that other public officials, including legislators, respect those rights. For two centuries American judges have ruled both national and state legislation invalid because it invaded the rights of freedom of speech or religion or of the due process of law or of the equal protection of law that the United States Constitution recognizes. Since World War II, many other democracies have adopted that practice—it is a central feature of both the provisional and proposed final constitution in the new South Africa, for example. British citizens, however, still cannot challenge legislation in British courts on the ground that it violates their fundamental liberties. They can challenge their own Parliament in an international court—the European Court of Human Rights (ECHR)—because Britain has entered into a treaty giving its citizens that power. But the process is forbiddingly expensive and lengthy. Why shouldn't British citizens be able to defend their rights at home?

It would be too complacent to think that these rights do not need defending. I do not mean that Britain has become a police state. Citizens are free openly to criticize the government, and the government does not kidnap or torture or kill its opponents. But liberty has nevertheless been under threat in Britain for the last few decades by a notable decline in the *culture* of liberty—the community's shared sense that individual privacy and dignity and freedom of speech and conscience are crucially important and that they

---

[1] Ronald Dworkin is Professor of Jurisprudence at Oxford University.

are worth considerable sacrifices in official convenience or public expense to protect. Of course any democratic government must balance the interests and demands of different sections of the public and choose policies they think best for the community as a whole. It must therefore restrain people's freedom in various ways. It must lay down rules regulating how fast or in what direction people may drive, the size and character of the buildings they may build, the terms on which they may hire or fire employees, when and how they may merge or combine their businesses, and thousands of other matters.

In a culture of liberty, however, the public shares a sense, almost as a matter of secular religion, that certain freedoms are in principle exempt from this ordinary process of balancing and regulation. It insists that government may not dictate its citizens' convictions or tastes, or decide what they say or hear or read or write, or deny them a fair trial by historical standards, even when it believes, with however good reason, that infringing these liberties would on balance protect security or promote economy or efficiency or convenience. In a culture of liberty, these freedoms cannot be abridged except to prevent a clear and serious danger—a calamity—and even then only so far as is absolutely necessary to prevent it.

Of course difficult questions arise about exactly which activities should belong to the protected system of liberties, about how clear and present a particular danger is, and about when less stringent means of regulation than censorship or prohibition are available. People equally committed to freedom disagree about whether, for example, the dangers of tobacco advertising or the offensiveness of racial epithets justify withholding protection from these forms of speech. The essence of liberty is not agreement over particular hard cases, however, but an attitude: that the traditional liberties are so crucial to human dignity that hard questions should be decided in their favor as far as possible, that a fence should be constructed around and at some distance from the heartland of free expression, privacy, and fair criminal process, that government should bear the onus of demonstrating that *any* interference with *any* part of the fundamental liberties is really necessary to secure some essential goal.

That is the spirit in which a culture of liberty approaches hard questions about speech and protest and the right to silence and the rights of minorities. It does not ask whether the public will be more or less pleased, on the whole, if there is less sex on television. Or whether the loss of valuable information to the public will outbalance the gain to the security system if television programs about Gibraltar or Northern Ireland are censored, or whether government operates more smoothly and efficiently when public officials are prosecuted for leaking embarrassing information, or whether there will be less crime if suspects are henceforth denied the right of silence.

These questions are unfair to liberty, because the value of liberty cannot be measured piecemeal, in iotas of information sacrificed or imagination stifled or creativity impaired or innocent people convicted. Measured case-by-case against the immediate aims of ordinary politics, the value of liberty will always seem speculative and marginal; it will always seem academic, abstract, and dispensable. Liberty is already lost, whatever the outcome, as soon as old freedoms are put at risk in cost-benefit politics. A decent nation is committed to freedom in a different way. It knows that liberty's value lies on a different scale, that invading freedom is not a useful technique of government but a compromise of the nation's dignity and civilization. In the last decades, on the other hand, British government has too often treated freedom as just another commodity, to be enjoyed when there is no particular political or commercial or administrative price to be paid for it, but abandoned, with no evident grief, when the price begins to rise. That is not despotism. But it cheapens liberty and diminishes the nation.

A Bill of Rights for Britain?

When the eminent French historian François Furet lectured in Britain on the occasion of the bicentennial of the French Revolution, he said that the signal triumph of democracy in our time is the growing acceptance and enforcement of a crucial idea: that democracy is not the same thing as majority rule, and that in a real democracy liberty and minorities have legal protection in the form of a written constitution that even Parliament cannot change to suit its whim or policy. Under that vision of democracy, a bill of individual constitutional rights is part of fundamental law, and judges, who are not elected and who are therefore removed from the pressures of partisan politics, are responsible for interpreting and enforcing that Bill of Rights as they are for all other parts of the legal system.

The United Sates was born committed to that idea of democracy, and now every member of the European Community except Britain accepts it, and so do the great majority of other mature democracies, including India, Canada, and almost all the other democratic Commonwealth nations. Britain stands alone in insisting that Parliament must have absolutely unlimited legal power to do anything it wishes.

British constitutional lawyers once bragged that a constitutional Bill of Rights was unnecessary because in Britain the people can trust the rulers they elect. But now a great many people—more than ever before—believe that this is no longer true, and that the time has come for Britain to join other democracies and put its Parliament under law. Would a charter of constitutional rights help restore the British culture of liberty? Learned

Hand, a great American constitutional judge, said that when the spirit of freedom dies in a people, no constitution or Supreme Court can bring it back to life. And it is true that many nations with formal constitutional guarantees, including some of the European nations that have made the European Convention of Human Rights part of their own law, fail fully to honour their constitutional rights in practice. But though a written constitution is certainly not a sufficient condition for liberty to thrive again in Britain, it may well be a necessary one.

Of course the idea of a Bill Rights is rejected by those politicians who are anxious to protect their own power when in office. Many Tory politicians, and even some Labour ones, think that their government is now too much rather than too little hedged in by judges. They howl whenever judges find the actions of ministers and officials illegal, as judges have done several times in recent years, and they call for Parliament to change the law to keep the judges off their backs. More and more politicians are now coming to support to the idea of a Bill of Rights enforceable by judges, however, and new support for that idea has emerged within the general public, from people demanding the rights and liberties that in other countries belong to them, not to the politicians.

How could a genuine British Bill of Rights, enforceable by British judges, be created? One way would be remarkably simple. As I said earlier, Britain is already committed by international treaty to a charter of constitutional rights called the European Convention on Human Rights. With very little procedural fuss Parliament could enact a statute providing that the principles of that convention are henceforth part of the law of Britain, enforceable by British judges in British courts. In fact, bills to that effect have been introduced in Parliament on several occasions in recent years, and though these were defeated on each occasion, the prospects that such a law might be enacted have improved steadily, from none to negligible to substantial.

The European Convention was adopted in 1950, when the memory of Fascist tyranny was fresh, and it has now been signed by all the nations of Western Europe. Under the treaty, an individual citizen in each of the member countries has the right, when he or she thinks his nation has broken some covenant of the Convention, to bring a complaint before the European Commission. If the Commission decides that the individual has satisfied procedural requirements, and that his complaint is not manifestly ill-founded, it begins an investigation and at the same time attempts a friendly settlement between the individual and his or her government. If no friendly settlement is reached, and the Commission decides that a violation has occurred, it may assign the matter to the judges of the European Court of Human Rights (ECHR) in Strasbourg, and if that Court agrees that the Convention has been violated, it orders the offending nation to change its laws to bring them into accord with what the Convention requires.

Britain has been a frequent defendant before the ECHR, as one might expect, given its recent insensitivity to individual freedom. Since 1965 twice as many petitions have been lodged against it as against any other member, and it has lost more serious cases than any other nation. The ECHR has ordered Britain to stop inhuman and degrading treatment of suspected terrorists, to allow prisoners access to a lawyer while in jail, to stop birching as a punishment in the Isle of Man and caning as a punishment in State schools, to repeal certain laws against homosexuality in Northern Ireland, to end the worst forms of discrimination in immigration, to improve the legal rights of prisoners and mental patients, and to adopt protection against indiscriminate wiretapping and covert surveillance.

In theory, then, Britain already has a constitution of individual rights, enforceable by a court in Strasbourg, which Parliament is powerless to abridge except in a case of emergency. But, as I suggested, the European Convention is no substitute for a domestic Bill of Rights interpreted and enforced by British judges trained in British traditions. A private citizen who feels his rights under the Convention have been violated must first exhaust whatever remedies might be thought to be available at home, and then prepare and argue a case first before the European Commission and then, if matters go that far, before the ECHR. The process is fearsomely expensive (there is, for all practical purposes, no legal aid available) and takes on average six years, by which time, particularly in cases involving censorship, the issue is almost always academic.

All the other major European countries have made the Convention part of their domestic law, so that it can be raised and its benefit claimed in national courts. But Britain has not done so. Some British judges believe that they nevertheless have the power, and indeed the responsibility, to take the principles of the Convention into account in interpreting British law. Several judges in the *Spycatcher* litigation, for example, said that when British law is unclear, it should be read so as to be consistent with Article 10 of the Convention, which declares that a member nation may not abridge free speech, except as is 'necessary in a democratic society'. Some judges go further, and accept a general presumption that Parliament does not intend to violate the Convention, or to permit ministers to do so, unless the plain language of some statute indicates otherwise, and that ministers must therefore exercise the general powers granted by statutes only in ways the Convention permits.

But even those judges who are ready to give effect to the Convention by way of a presumption about parliamentary intent cannot do so when a statute or the common law is not vague or ambiguous but expressly requires what the Convention prohibits. The Prevention of Terrorism Act, which allows suspects to be held for a week without being charged, is not unclear. Nor is the Public Order Act which gives the police unjustified control over

protest marches. Nor is the legislation abolishing the ancient right to silence. Judges have no power to protect the people from such statutes, even
if the judges think the statutes are plain violations of Britain's international
obligations under the European Convention.

If Parliament made the European Convention part of British law judges
could decide on their own whether some official action or parliamentary
statute violated the Convention. They could decide that question in the
same way they decide any other issue of law. So any statute that might be
thought to violate the fundamental rights that Britain is committed by
treaty to respect could be challenged at once and not six or more years later
when the government's aim of stopping public access to information, for
example, has long since been achieved anyway. Official denials of privacy,
or of the right of legitimate protest, or of the rights of people accused of
crimes, could be challenged at once, and not years later when the damage
was done and long past undoing.

If the judges used this new authority well, the most important and immediate benefit would be a revitalization of the liberty and dignity of the
people. Government and officials would no longer be so free to keep secrets
from the people they are supposed to serve, or to ignore rights the nation
has a solemn obligation to respect. Other, more speculative but in the long
run equally important, benefits might then follow. The European Convention speaks in abstract terms, and subjects many of the rights it declares to
equally abstract exceptions. Article 8, for example, which declares that
everyone has the right to respect for his private and family life, home and
correspondence, allows an exception for measures 'necessary in a democratic society in the interests of national security, public safety or the
economic well-being of the country', or 'necessary for the protection of
health and morals'. Different lawyers take different views about what such
phrases mean. British judges could not adopt a *less* generous interpretation
of these abstract clauses than the ECHR has established in its own decisions; a British court could not deny rights the ECHR had recognized. But
British judges could certainly adopt, for Britain, a *more* generous interpretation, using the rich and special traditions of the British common law to
develop out of the Convention a particularly British view of the fundamental rights of citizens in a democratic society. They might decide, for example, that Article 6 of the Convention, which requires 'fair' criminal trials,
should be interpreted to require nations to observe guarantees established
in their own legal traditions, which in the case of Britain would include the
right to silence.

If British judges began to create as well as follow constitutional jurisprudence in that way, their decisions would be bound to influence the Commission and the ECHR, as well as the courts of the other nations who have
signed the Convention, and, indeed, of all the other nations across the globe

who are now wrestling with the problem of making abstract human rights concrete. Incorporation would but the special skills of British lawyers and judges, and the heritage of British legal principle, at the service of the civilized world. Britain could become once again a leader in defining and protecting individual freedom, instead of, as a sullen defendant, giving ground to liberty only when ordered to do so by a foreign court.

Law and lawyers might then begin to play a different, more valuable role in society than they now even aspire to. The courts, charged with the responsibility of creating form the Convention a distinctly British scheme of human rights and liberty, might think more in terms of principle and less in terms of narrow precedent. University law courses and faculties might develop in the same direction, trying to produce a legal profession that could be the conscience, not just the servant, of government and industry. Different men and women might then be tempted to the law as a career, and from their ranks a more committed and idealistic generation of judges might emerge, encouraging a further cycle in the renaissance of liberty. No part of this attractive chain reaction would be inevitable, of course, even if Britain did decide in some way to incorporate the European Convention into its domestic law. But it is hard to imagine a political decision more likely to set it off.

How Could the Convention be Incorporated?

The European Convention is not a perfect Bill of Rights for Britain. It was a compromise drafted to accommodate a variety of nations with different legal systems and traditions; it is in many ways weaker than the American Bill of Rights; and it is hedged about with vague limitations and powerful escape clauses of different sorts. The Convention does protect liberty better than it is now protected by Parliament alone, however, as recent history shows. It protects freedom of speech, religion and expression, privacy, and the most fundamental rights of accused criminals, and it grants indirect but effective way rights against discrimination. Since Britain is already subject to the Convention as a matter of both moral obligation and international law, it would plainly be easier to enact that charter into British law, substantially as it is, perhaps with clarifying changes and additions from other international covenants Britain has also signed, than to begin drafting and debating a wholly new Bill of Rights. Even if it were possible to adopt an entirely new set of rights, the European Convention would remain law enforceable before the ECHR, and the potential conflict between the two fundamental charters of rights might be a source of wasteful confusion.

So those who love liberty should unite in supporting the incorporation of the Convention. But how can this be done, and in what form should it be done? Suppose Parliament declared tomorrow that both its own past and future statutes and the acts of ministers and officials under them shall be null and void unless they are in conformity with the Convention's principles. Would not a future Parliament, tired of that constraint, have the power simply to repeal the incorporation? Indeed, would it not repeal the incorporation automatically whenever it enacted a statute inconsistent with the Convention, in which case incorporation would be a nonsense form the start? Suppose Parliament tomorrow both incorporated the Convention *and* provided that the incorporation could not be repealed by a future Parliament except by an extraordinary majority of, say, three-quarters of the members. Could not a future Parliament, by ordinary majority vote, simply repeal the provision requiring an extraordinary majority?

Many lawyers assume that it could. When Roy Hattersley was Deputy Leader of the Labour Party, for example, he defended his opposition to a Bill of Rights on the ground, among others, that even if Parliament incorporated the European Convention unanimously, a future Parliament could simply repeal the incorporation any time it proved inconvenient. In any case, the popular legal thesis that one Parliament cannot limit the power of future Parliaments is undefended and seems, on re-examination, wrong in law. It assumes that any Parliament has the legal power to do absolutely anything it wishes to do, notwithstanding what earlier Parliaments have done. What is the authority for that proposition? It plainly does not owe *its* authority to any parliamentary decision, because it would beg the question for Parliament to decide that its own power was unlimited.

British lawyers say that Parliament is an absolute sovereign because that seems (for most of them intuitively and unreflectively) the best interpretation of British legal history, practice, and tradition. But legal history and practice can change with great speed. Suppose a national debate on constitutional principle took place, after which Parliament declared that the European Convention was incorporated into British law, and also declared that this decision could itself be repealed or amended only by a special procedure requiring an extraordinary majority of both Houses. Then British constitutional history would have been altered just by that decision having been made, understood and accepted by the public as a whole. Practice and tradition would have changed, and the old interpretation, which declares absolute parliamentary supremacy, would plainly no longer fit. Judges would have no legal or logical reason not to hold future Parliaments to the decision the nation had made. They would have no legal or logical reason not to insist that only an extraordinary majority could restore the present situation.

So the popular argument that there is no way Parliament can impose a constitutional Bill of Rights on a later Parliament is at least dubious. But notice that I have so far been discussing what might be called a *strong* form of incorporation, which provides that any statute inconsistent with the Convention is null and void. Several influential supporters of a Bill of Rights (including Lord Scarman, a former Lord of Appeal in Ordinary, who has been a pioneer in the argument for incorporation) have proposed that in the first instance incorporation should take what is technically a weaker form: the incorporating statute should provide that an inconsistent statute is null and void unless Parliament has expressly stated that it *intends* the statute to override the Convention. In practice this technically weaker version of incorporation would probably provide almost as much protection as the stronger one. If a government conceded that its statute violated the Convention would have no defence before the Commission or the ECHR. Quite apart from that practical point, no respectable government would wish to announce that it did not care whether its legislation or decisions violated the country's domestic promises and international obligations. If a government felt itself able to able to make such an announcement, except in the most extraordinary circumstances, the spirit of liberty would be dead anyway, beyond the power of any constitution to revive. At least in the first instance, therefore, the weaker form of incorporation would be acceptable if no stronger form was politically feasible.

Should Parliament be Supreme?

That is the case for incorporating the European Convention into domestic British law. It is no mystery, as I said, that many politicans are reluctant to accept that case. Ministers and officials are rarely keen to justify themselves before judges, and constitutional rights often make important political objectives more difficult to achieve. These are the costs of a culture of liberty, and politicians, above all, are often reluctant to pay them. What is surprising, however, is the weakness of the arguments that these politicians and others have deployed *against* incorporation. In the rest of this essay, I shall consider all the arguments of which I am aware.

Opponents say that the very idea of a Bill of Rights restricting the power of Parliament is hostile to the British tradition that Parliament not judges should be sovereign. That supposed tradition of Parliamentary supremecy seems less appealing now, when a very powerful executive and well-disciplined political parties mean less effective power for backbench MPs, than it did before these developments. The tradition has already been compromised in recent decades, moreover. It was altered by the European Communities Act, for example, under which judges have the power to override Parliamentary decisions in order to enforce directly effective Community rules. In any case, incorporating the European Convention would not diminish Parliament's present power in any way that could

reasonably be thought objectionable, since Parliament is already constrained by that Convention. If the Convention were incorporated in what
I have called the strong form, under which a future Parliament would not
have the legal power to violate the Convention even if it expressly said it
intended to do so, then the power of Parliament might be somewhat more
limited than it is now, because British judges might develop a special British
interpretation of the Convention that in some cases recognized individual
constitutional rights which the ECHR would not recognize. It is hard to
argue that this further limitation would be wrong in principle, however.
Britain agreed , when it accepted the European Convention and the jurisdiction of the European Court of Human Rights, that it would be bound by
the principles laid down in the convention as these principles were interpreted not by Parliament but by the judges of that court. If that limitation
on the power of Parliament is acceptable, how can it be unacceptable that
it be limited by the same principles as interpreted and applied not by mainly
foreign judges but by British judges trained in the common law and in the
legal and political traditions of their own country?

   The argument from Parliamentary supremacy would be irrelevant,
moreover, if the Convention were incorporated in the weaker form I suggested should be the initial goal. For then Parliament could override the
Convention by mere majority vote, provided it was willing expressly to
concede its indifference about doing so. No doubt that condition would, in
practice, prevent a government from introducing legislation it might otherwise enact. That is the point of incorporation, even in the weak form. But
forcing Parliament to make the choice between obeying its international
obligations and admitting that it is violating them does not limit Parliament's supremacy, but only its capacity for duplicity. Candour is hardly
inconsistent with sovereignty.

Is Incorporation Undemocratic?

The argument from parliamentary supremacy is often thought to rest on
a more important and fundamental argument, however, according to
which Britain should not have subscribed to the European Convention in
the first place. This is the argument from democracy: that it is undemocratic
for appointed judges rather than an elected Parliament to have the last
word about what the law is. People who take that view will resist incorporation, because incorporation enlarges the practical consequences of what
they regard as the mistake of accepting the Convention. They will certainly
resist the idea that domestic judges should have the power to read the
Convention more liberally and so provide more protection than the ECHR
requires.

Their argument misunderstands what democracy is, however. In the first place, it confuses democracy with the power of elected officials. There is no genuine democracy, even though officials have been elected in otherwise fair elections, unless voters have had access to the information they need so that their votes can be knowledgeable choices rather than merely manipulated responses to advertising campaigns. Citizens of a democracy must be able to participate in government not just spasmodically, in elections from time to time, but constantly through informed and free debate about their government's performance between elections. Those evident requirements suggest what other nations have long ago realized: that Parliament *must* be constrained in certain ways in order that democracy be genuine rather than sham. The argument that a Bill of Rights would be undemocratic is therefore not just wrong but the opposite of the truth.

The depressing story of the Thatcher government's concentrated assault on free speech is more than enough to prove that point. In the *Harman*, *Ponting*, and *Spycatcher* cases, in denying a public interest exception in the new Official Secrets Act, in the broadcasting bans, in the *Death on the Rock* matter, government tried to censor information of the type citizens need in order to vote intelligently or criticise officials effectively. The officials who took these decisions acted out of various motives: out of concern for confidentiality, or to discourage views they thought dangerous, or to improve the morale of the police and security services, or sometimes just to protect themselves from political damage. But none of these reasons is good enough because in a democracy officials have no right to dictate what the voters should know or think. The politicians would very likely have acted differently in every one of these cases if Article 10 of the European Convention had been part of British law, and the prospect of judicial intervention had been immediate and certain rather than speculative and delayed. British democracy would obviously have been strengthened not weakened as a result.

It is true, however, that the European Convention forbids governments to adopt or retain some laws that a majority of their citizens do want, and would continue to want even if they had all the information anyone might wish. The ECHR struck down Northern Ireland's homosexuality law, for example, not because the Court doubted that a majority of the voters of Northern Ireland wanted that law, but because the Convention prohibits that form of discrimination whether the majority wishes it or not. If the European Convention were incorporated, British judges might strike down Britain's blasphemy law, which prohibits books or art deeply offensive to conventional Christianity, even if a majority favoured retaining that law. The blasphemy law violates Articles 9 and 10 of the Convention, which protect freedom of conscience and free speech. In my view (although British courts have rejected the suggestion) the blasphemy law also violates

Articles 9 and 14, which taken together prohibit religious discrimination, because that law discriminates in favour of Christianity. Some Muslims said it was unjust that Salman Rushdie's book, *The Satanic Verses*, could not be prosecuted as blasphemous of their religion. Of course the blasphemy law should not be extended to other religions, as they argued it should. It should instead be repealed, because it would violate the Convention even if it applied to religion in general.

Would it offend democracy if a British court had the power to strike down the blasphemy law as inconsistent with the Convention? No, because true democracy is not just *statistical* democracy, in which anything a majority or plurality wants is legitimate for that reason, but *communal* democracy, in which a majority decision is legitimate only if it is a majority within a community of equals.[2] This means not only that everyone must be allowed to participate in politics as an equal, through the vote and through freedom of speech and protest, but that political decisions must treat everyone with equal concern and respect, that each individual person must be guaranteed fundamental civil and political rights which no combination of other citizens can take away, no matter how numerous they are or how much they despise his or her race or morals or way of life. This view of what democracy means is at the heart of all the charters of human rights, including the European Convention. It is the mature, principled conception that has now triumphed in South Africa as well as throughout Western Europe and North America, and it is the explicit goal of the democratic reformers of Eastern Europe. The rival, statistical conception of democracy, according to which democracy is consistent with denying fundamental rights if the majority approves, was the ideal proclaimed by the Communist tyrannies after the Second World War: they said democracy meant government in the interests of the masses. The civilized world has recoiled from that totalitarian view, and the idea that protecting constitutional rights against majority will is undemocratic must be abandoned along with it.

This seems to me a decisive answer to the argument that incorporation would be undemocratic. I believe that a different but equally decisive answer can also be made in Britain now: that the argument is self-defeating because the great majority of British people rejects the crude statistical view of democracy on which the argument is based. Even people who do not think of themselves as belonging to any minority have good reasons for insisting that a majority's power to rule should be limited. Something crucially important to them—their religious freedom or professional independence or liberty of conscience, for example—might one day prove inconvenient to the government of the day. Even people who cannot imag-

---

[2] The distinction between the statistical and communal conceptions of democracy, and the case for the latter, are discussed at length in my book, i.e. *Freedom's Law* (Oxford University Press, 1996).

ine being isolated in that way might prefer to live in a genuine political community, in which everyone's dignity as an equal is protected, rather than just in a State which they control.

That attractive impulse lies dormant in day-to-day political argument about how to fight terrorism or whether tolerance for homosexuals should be promoted with taxpayers' money or when suspected criminals' telephones should be tapped. But it might well surface during a general constitutional debate, when the nation reflects abut its traditions and its image of itself. A public opinion poll in Britain in 1986, taken before a parliamentary debate about incorporation, reported that twice as many of those questioned favoured incorporation as opposed it, and that 71 per cent thought a constitutional Bill of Rights would improve democracy. Such polls are unreliable in various ways, but the dramatic preference for incorporation is nevertheless impressive. Britain will not have a Bill of Rights, even in the weak form I described, unless it turns out, after an intense period of public debate, that the preference is genuine, that the British people do share a constitutional sense of justice. If so, and if we assume that this sense of justice will be shared by their descendants, then the argument that incorporation is undemocratic will have been defeated on its own terms.

Will the Judges Have to Work Too Hard?

The remaining objections I shall consider appeal not to philosophical principles about parliamentary supremacy or democracy or the superiority of ordinary legislation, but to more practical problems associated with the British judicial system. I begin with the most surprising of these. It is said that British judges are already overworked, and that asking them to consider constitutional questions as well as the ordinary legal claims they now entertain would impose far too great a burden on them. Some judges themselves make that argument: in a television discussion some years ago every judge who spoke against the proposal (some spoke for it) gave that as his reason. But the fear of overwork is surely exaggerated. Canadian judges complained of overwork when the Canadian Charter of Human Rights was first adopted, but most of them now concede that the additional work is becoming manageable.

I do not doubt that if the Convention did became part of British internal law, enterprising lawyers would make constitutional claims in a wide variety of criminal and even civil proceedings. It would cost their clients little for them to add, to any other claim or defence they make to a criminal action, for example, that the police used unconscionable methods forbidden by Article 6 of the Convention, that the punishment threatened is inhuman or degrading and so contrary to Article 3, that the statute in question in some way abridges freedom of expression contrary to Article 10 or infringes privacy contrary to Article 8, or some other charge under some other article. Judges would, of course, have to consider any such claim. But they would soon gain experience in constitutional matters quickly enough to see which of such claims had no merit. The decisions of the ECHR would be available, and British precedents would soon begin to build up, in the normal common law manner. Judges have a variety of traditional techniques for disposing of frivolous arguments in a way that makes counsel less likely to repeat them, moreover, and foolish civil litigation is discouraged by the normal practice that the loser must pay the winner's costs.

But suppose the fear of judicial overwork were well-founded. Suppose that even after plainly unmeritorious claims had been weeded out, constitutional issues took up so much judicial time that the overall legal system did suffer from clogging and lack of time for other matters. That would mean that the situation of freedom and justice in Britain is even worse than advocates of a Bill of Rights fear. It would then be preposterous to complain that it would have been better to save judges the work than to ask them to help defend the fundamental rights of British citizens. The appropriate solution—the only defensible solution—would then be to strengthen the judiciary. If nothing else worked, more judges could be appointed—there is no lack of qualified senior lawyers. But it is far from clear that new judges would be required. The British judicial system is famously underfinanced and inefficient: even the most senior judges are given next to no secretarial, library, or other assistance. In America every judge in the federal system, and almost every judge in the higher state courts, is assisted by at least one full-time paid clerk, and justices of the Supreme Court, which has the greatest burden of constitutional cases, each have the use of at least two clerks. These law clerks are generally recent and distinguished graduates of law schools, who serve as clerks for one or two years before beginning their own professional or academic careers. They are fresh from a more intense study of constitutional issues in law school than most judges have time to pursue on their own. Several British judges who are familiar with the American practice are already anxious to move some way towards it, and would be particularly ready to do so if their work were expanded by incorporating the European Convention into British law.

The cost would be minimal, and the benefits in judicial imagination, improved training of the lawyers who became law clerks, and improved connections between the academic legal world and the bench would be significant, quite apart from the value of the practice in assisting judges asked to undertake a new department of work. Any problem of judicial overload could therefore be cured if the government were to spend more money on justice, by appointing new judges or allowing the present judges to use their time better. So the argument that incorporation would overwork the judges is actually an argument based on stinginess, a particularly debased form of the bad idea that rights should be denied when it is expensive or otherwise inconvenient to recognize them.

Are the Judges Up to the Job?

If even the weak version of incorporating the European Convention were adopted, judges would have more power than they do now. The additional power would be a matter of degree rather than of kind, because, as I said, some judges already appeal to the Convention as an aid to interpreting the will of Parliament, and because under the weak version of incorporation Parliament would have ultimate power to oust the jurisdiction of the judges, if it were willing to declare its intention not to respect the Convention. But the increase in the judges' role would be significant even if only quantitative, and that provokes an objection which is thought particularly powerful on the left of British politics.

It claims that British judges are, as a group, drawn from a very narrow and privileged section of the community, that they are insensitive or hostile to the interests and convictions of the rest of the nation, that they have for generations shown a collective bias for property and the middle class and against the trades-union movement, and that they therefore cannot be trusted with the increased political power that incorporation, even in a weak form, would give them. This generalization about British judges is, in my view, both very exaggerated and out-of-date, but it does have an historical foundation. Judges are drawn from the Bar, which remains an élitist profession, and an unconscionably high percentage of them are Oxbridge graduates, some of whom have found it difficult to abandon conventional wisdom and attitudes. But the Tory outrage of recent years, against judgments exercising judicial review of official decisions, is evidence of a change, and many British judges, including some of the most influential Law Lords, have political and social attitudes very different from those of the old stereotype.

Moreover the argument that British judges cannot be trusted with constitutional rights makes an obviously untenable assumption: that judges will remain the same kinds of people, and decide cases in the same kinds of way, whether or not they are asked to enforce a Bill of constitutional rights. If the Convention were incorporated into British law, even the most legally conservative judges would believe themselves bound to apply that decision in the spirit in which it was taken; in any case they would know they were obliged, by the act of incorporation, to have regard to decisions of the ECHR. The legal culture would have changed around them: legal education and professional literature and debate would be based on new assumptions. In time, as I said earlier, the character of the Bar and then the Bench might well change in consequence. If the experiment worked, different men and women from different backgrounds would want to be lawyers, and these would include many more who were attracted to law as an instrument of social justice. They would be trained differently, in a more international and cosmopolitan style, taught by a law faculty engaged in a different kind of research. Judges would soon begin to be drawn from a very different and much more diverse and exciting profession.

Suppose all this is wrong, however, and too many judges continue to be insensitive to the values of liberty and equality. How much would have been lost by incorporation then? Opponents warn that conservative judges are 'executive-minded' and so would take Parliament or the government's side against individuals. But even in that case—even if all judges making constitutional decisions took the government's side—nothing would have been *lost* by incorporation, because judges would then simply have failed to exercise a power they had been given. It can hardly be thought a strong argument against giving judges useful power that some of them might refuse to exercise it. Judges who refused to check ministers and officials or to set aside Parliamentary statutes would simply be leaving the legal world as it would have been without incorporation. At worst nothing would have been lost, and it is extremely unlikely that nothing would have been gained. Some judges would exercise their new power well even if most did not, and the profession and the public would have a new basis for criticizing and educating the laggards. Litigants who were denied their rights in decisions the profession criticized would be more likely to appeal to the ECHR, and the Court would hand down decisions that even the most conservative judges would then be obliged to follow in future cases.

It is odd how often all is misunderstood. Lawyers hostile to incorporation warn, for example, that it would be unwise to entrust a constitutional guaranty of free speech to British judges, who in the past have shown themselves insensitive to that right. But even if the judges did no more to protect speech under a clear constitutional direction than they did without it, which is implausible, the situation would not be worse than if they had not been directed at all. Other lawyers point to the fact that the American Supreme Court did not stop the American government from interning citizens of Japanese extraction after Pearl Harbor, or prevent Senator McCarthy's short reign of terror during the Red-scare witch-hunts. These are indeed conspicuous failures in the Supreme Court's long and on the whole creditable record. But they of course furnish no argument for the thesis that the Supreme Court should not have had the powers it did not on those occasions use.

Some lawyers worry, however, not that conservative judges would defer too much to other political institutions, but that they would, on the contrary, interfere in government by preventing some reforming government of the future from radical changes that would genuinely be needed in the interests of further equality and justice. Lawyers who voice this fear call attention to decisions of the Supreme Court in the early 1930s which held important parts of Franklin Roosevelt's New Deal social legislation unconstitutional, until the 'Nine Old Men' of that Court gave way, by death and retirement, to new appointments. A careful reading of the European Convention should reassure those who are worried by that analogy, however. The Convention was adopted by governments several of which had already embarked on welfare-state programmes. It contains a specific guarantee of the right to form and join trades unions, and no provision that any judge, no matter how conservative, could use to strike down legislation that a responsible egalitarian government would sponsor.

In its very conservative period—during the early New Deal and for decades before—the Supreme Court cited the Fifth Amendment to the United States Constitution, which provides that Congress may not deprive anyone of liberty or property without due process of law, to hold progressive legislation unconstitutional. In 1905 the Court held, for example, that a New York law limiting the number of hours bakers could be asked to work each week deprived both bakers and their employers of the 'liberty' of contract. That use of the due process clause was legally indefensible, as even the most conservative American lawyers now almost all agree. But in any case there is no comparable clause in the European Convention. The first protocol does provide that no one shall be deprived of 'possessions' except in accordance with principles of international law, and that States must 'respect the right of parents to secure . . . education and teaching in accordance with their own religious and philosophical convictions'. It has already been established, through decisions of the ECHR, that these provisions would not permit a British government to confiscate private property with no compensation, or to abolish independent schools. (Britain accepted an even clearer prohibition on abolishing independent schools when it ratified the International Covenant on Civil and Political Rights in 1976.) But the protocol leaves ample room for social legislation any responsible government would wish to enact; it insists, for example, that a State may 'control the use of property in accordance with the public interest', and it does not oppose obvious measures that would decrease the unfair advantages of private schooling. The risk is therefore inconsequential that after incorporation judges would be able to stop social and economic changes that a future government of the Left would actually want, and that a decent respect for individual dignity would permit it to make.

Would Judges Become Politicians?

The last objection in my catalogue argues that if judges had the power to set aside legislation as unconstitutional, judicial appointments would become undesirably political, and judges would be thought politicians themselves. British judges already make politically sensitive decisions: they review the legality of executive actions, for example, and interpret and apply trades union law. Opponents of incorporation argue that allowing judges an explicit power to declare statutes invalid would make their political role greater and more apparent, and therefore reduce confidence in the independence of the judiciary. They remember the heavily televised national debate and partisan contest over Reagan's nomination of Judge Robert Bork to the Supreme Court in 1987, and shudder when they contemplate a comparable public squabble over judicial appointments in Britain.

That nomination battle was most extraordinary even in America, and it was provoked by Reagan's decision to appoint a judge who had made himself a political figure already. (Bork had for many years campaigned among right-wing groups for his own nomination, promising in articles and speeches that he would revolutionize constitutional law. He denounced, and suggested that he would vote to overrule, a great number of well-established Supreme Court decisions that Americans had come to think of as the core of civil rights and racial justice in the United States.) In any case, there are important differences between the way judicial appointments are made in Britain and the United States—in the United States the appointment of any federal judge requires Senate approval, for example—which make a public nomination fight much more unlikely in Britain.

Nevertheless incorporation might well have the consequence of focusing more attention on judicial appointments there. If judges had the additional powers that incorporating the European Convention would give them, the public would presumably have more interest in who the judges were, and the media would have that incentive for examining the qualifications of controversial appointees. So would academic lawyers, public interest groups and professional committees. A government whose judicial appointments did not follow the established pattern of selecting among barristers with the highest professional qualifications could expect the public to notice and strongly to disapprove. These are not, however, evident disadvantages. On the contrary, an increased public interest in and scrutiny of high judicial officials would better serve a culture of liberty.

Conclusion

Constitutional political events—whether these are formal like Magna Carta and the Glorious Revolution or informal like the New Deal in America—

define a nation's character in symbolism that cannot be fully appreciated at the time. The long Tory administration of the 1980s and 1990s will have been a constitutional event for liberty, one way or another, whatever happens. If the country acquiesces in freedom's decline, if censorship and intimidation and surveillance and the curtailment of ancient liberties generate no outrage but only indifference, if a complacent establishment calms itself with the false comfort that things are 'not so bad' or 'have never been all that much better', then the country will have lost a heritage not easily regained. If, on the other hand, a new constitutional debate galvanizes the British citizenry into a new concern for its old rights, and that concern is recognised and symbolised in a new constitutional charter, Britain will have announced that its culture of liberty is too valuable to trade for convenience or economy or repose. It will have taken a crucial step back towards its old place at the frontiers of personal freedom.

7

Ideas Whose Time Has Passed

BILL EMMOTT AND DAVID MANASIAN[1]

The trouble with constitutional arguments is that they are both less important than those who engage in them think, and more important than the cynics believe. By changing a constitution, you cannot with a wave of a wand alter the political culture and behaviour of a nation. This is not, however, a reason to dismiss the idea of constitutional change. At the heart of many real political grievances and weaknesses constitutional problems can be found, or else problems susceptible to a constitutional solution. It is on such grievances and weaknesses that the case for a Bill of Rights, and other constitutional reforms, must rest.

Constitutional debate is not something to which Britons are accustomed. People do not march down London streets to campaign for proportional representation. No one chains themselves to the railings of the House of Lords to plead for its abolition. The newspapers are not full of columns arguing the case for or against a Bill of Rights. Even when in October 1994 *The Economist* used its cover to declare itself in favour of the abolition of the monarchy it caused barely a flutter; a few hundred letters were received some of them passionate, several of them vitriolic, but the moment passed quickly without leaving much of a trace.

The reason for this lack of interest, it might plausibly be argued, is that the British are passably satisfied with their political freedoms. They may be contemptuous of politicians, cynical about abilities as well as the motives of MPs and ministers of either party, but they are truly afraid that constitutional change might threaten the stability of their daily lives. Only in places where people feel genuinely afraid and systematically repressed do constitutions and political frameworks become important, which is why Northern Ireland is the only real venue for constitutional dispute within the British Isles. Even in Scotland, where the desire for some sort of devolved power does exist, it is not a passion-raiser; devolution is far from the most important topic in Edinburgh or Glasgow, let alone the Western Isles.

It is true that there were times during Margaret Thatcher's period in government when this was not the case; people did take to the streets to

[1] Bill Emmott is editor of *The Economist*. David Manasian writes for *The Economist*.

protest about the poll tax, there were pitched battles between police and trade union members, and there was plenty of bar-room talk about Mrs Thatcher's dictatorial tendencies. But these moments too passed swiftly enough, and they did not come to any kind of a constitutional climax. So perhaps the traditional Tory assumption is true: wait patiently, let the British instincts for compromise and fair play emerge, and all will in the end be well.

That is an attractive view, until you notice what Tories themselves, traditional or otherwise, have been arguing about in recent years. For one issue, and one alone, has made a constitutional question a source of real, sustained political division and popular passion. This is Europe. For two decades, but especially in the past five years, Britain's relationship with the European Union has divided the Conservative Party in a thoroughly noticeable way; less noticeably, it has also divided popular opinion. Although a clear majority of those asked by opinion polls express support for British membership of the EU, large scores are also achieved by those decrying European intrusion, bureaucratic interference from Brussels, the transfer of powers to EU institutions, and so on.

There are, however, three important oddities about this. The first is that as part of this argument a whole barrow-load of grievances has been assembled and blamed, often wrongly, on Brussels. Two journalists, Christopher Booker and Richard North, have attained celebrity through their articles in the *Daily Telegraph* about the horrors of red tape and general bureaucratic intrusion: about bureaucrats trying to lay down the correct curvature for a cucumber, about bureaucrats forbidding pubs to put up signs directing customers to them, about butchers being forced to buy new equipment, or about patriots being forbidden to fly the Union Jack outside their houses. These stories have all formed part of a widespread movement of public opinion against the European Union.

The odd thing about this is that these grievances actually have very little to do with the European Union *per se*. They are in truth grievances about the citizen's lack of redress against over-mighty government, not merely of a general despotic sort but also of a petty bureaucratic variety. They are, in other words, evidence in favour of the introduction of a Bill of Rights.

That is an abstract idea, however, which is thus hard to grab hold of. Hostility to foreigners, in other words to Europe, is far easier to grasp. That is why the second oddity is that most ordinary people who bemoan the influence of Brussels do not really think they are entering a constitutional debate. To them, it is an issue of national independence, of sovereignty, of a preference for being governed by us rather than by them. This would be a banal observation, a recognition simply that Britons have no habit of constitutional debate and therefore do not recognize one when they have it, if it were not for the third oddity.

This is that, among the élite opinion which has campaigned against the loss of power to Brussels, namely, the Eurosceptic Tory MPs, the columnists on the *Daily Telegraph*, *The Times* and the *Daily Mail*, the constitutional principle on which their argument has been based has been exactly the wrong one. Their sacred principle is parliamentary sovereignty. They see the European Union as a violation of that principle, a threat to it. They do so in part for a good reason: the feeling that actions taken at the European level lack democratic support in many countries across the Union, but certainly in Britain.

But that point appears to blind them to a further, constitutionally more important one. This is that powers have not been stolen away from Parliament by a voracious, ambitious set of European institutions. Far from it, they have been given away by Britain's sovereign Parliament. And the moments when those powers were given away did not entail lengthy constitutional debate, consultation with whiskery constitutional experts, or complicated procedures designed to restrain hasty constitutional change such as referendums or 75 per cent votes of the Houses of Parliament. The accession to the European Communities in 1972, the Single European Act in 1986, the Maastricht treaty in 1993: all were passed by simple majorities of the House of Commons.

So the notion that there is a choice, a debate even, between parliamentary sovereignty and the federal European superstate is to ignore a contradiction and to miss the real costitutional point. The creation of what Europhobes see as a European superstate has been made possible by parliamentary sovereignty; the various transfers of powers were actions wholly in accordance with the British constitution. Even if a Eurosceptic Tory party were to repatriate powers from the European Union, the very next Parliament could transfer them back again, on a simple vote of the House of Commons. In terms of the only constitutional issue that has really exercised the British public and the British media in recent years, parliamentary sovereignty is certainly no the solution to it. It is the problem.

The Folly of Flexibility

In the past, many commentators have seen Parliament as the heart of Britain's constitutional solution: the concentration of power in the House of Commons, the epitome of Edmund Burke's view of representative government, gave Britain an ideal combination. On the one hand, the Commons was accountable to the people, in regular elections. On the other hand, however, the Commons had no need to worry about written constitutional principles, checks, or balances imposed by other institutions. Popular support for the British system was cultivated by the monarchy, which lent politics its necessary glamour, sense of tradition, and symbols of national unity. The Commons was therefore efficient; the government formed out of its majority had the great merit of strength.

Many parliamentarians still believe in this. They adore the idea of their own institution as the crucible of British democracy; they love to think that no idea has been suitably explored, or tested, until it has been revealed on the floor of the House of Commons. This view, however, comes up against an awkward truth. This is that the House of Commons itself is more or less moribund.

The days have gone when debates in the Commons were moments of great theatre, or even of great oratory. Most take place with few MPs in attendance. Hansard is barely consulted, let alone read. The Commons Select Committees, given new strength in reforms in the early 1980s, are of, at best, marginal importance. Once in a while, their view is noticed, and really counts. For the most part, however, they are a sideshow. And as for the House of Lords, the description of it by some of its peers as 'the land of the living dead' is cruel but apt: worthy though much of its activity is in scrutinizing legislation and holding debates in which many experts do participate, if the House of Lords was to disappear tomorrow it would make little practical difference.

A constitutional traditionalist would dispute this, both in terms of the judgment and its relevance. As that traditional view—crudely, 'if it ain't broke, don't fix it'—is the most widespread and powerful objection to reform, it is worth devoting time to it, even at the expense of delving into the history of constitutional writing and thinking.

Despite the anomalies and inconsistencies in Britain's constitution, the traditionalist would argue, the country is not obviously governed any worse than most other rich countries, and those countries all have their fair share of public discontent. Nor does it seem at all likely to tip into despotism. Particular policies and governments may prove unpopular from time to time. But Britain's parliamentary system of government has weathered vast social changes without the upheavals seen in many countries which have written constitutions. Most other nations have been forced to adopt these after military defeat, revolution, or political collapse. Britain is facing no such crisis. Small adjustments may have to be made occasionally, as in the past. But why overhaul a system which has taken more than 300 years to evolve, and whose accumulated wisdom has been admired and imitated throughout the world?

The trouble with this view is that it is based on a number of misconceptions, and relies on a misreading of Britain's own constitutional history. The key concepts pioneered by Britain which have had so much influence in the growth of democracy elsewhere—the separation of the executive, legislative, and judicial branches of government to provide institutional checks and balances, and fundamental rights protected from the encroachments of an overmighty government—were born of Parliament's battle to restrain the monarch in the seventeenth and eighteenth centuries, though never firmly established in Britain itself. In 1765 Sir William Blackstone, the leading English legal authority of the time, wrote that the total union of the executive and legislative branches of government 'would be productive of tyranny'.

Over the next century such a union is precisely what Britain achieved. The cabinet in effect assumed the executive role of the monarch. With the extension of the voting franchise to the middle and working classes and the rise of mass parties, the cabinet (and more particularly the prime minister) could stay in office only by exerting an iron discipline on its party supporters in the Commons, further concentrating power in its hands. By 1867 Walter Bagehot was praising the cabinet's control of nearly all government affairs, its 'near complete fusion of the executive and legislative powers' as the 'efficient secret' of the constitution.

When Albert Venn Dicey came to write *The Law of the Constitution* in 1885, the book which has set the parameters for most discussion about Britain's constitution ever since, the British system of government not only bore little resemblance to the written democratic constitutions being adopted elsewhere, but barely made intellectual sense. In Dicey's view the British constitution was based on two fundamental principles: the absolute sovereignty of Parliament and the rule of law. There is an inherent contradiction in this description. A truly sovereign parliament would be unconstrained even by the law which, of course, it would be free to change at any time.

In fact, on many occasions when the law—even the common law built up over centuries by the courts—has stood in the way of British governments, this is precisely what they have done. The judiciary assessing and ruling upon this law might be viewed as a separate branch of government. Individual judges, once appointed, are free from political meddling. But they are chosen in secret by the Lord Chancellor, a serving politician who acts as both head of the judiciary and a member of the cabinet.

Moreover, the powers of British judges are severely constrained. With no written constitution or Bill of Rights to guide them, they have lacked any legal authority to strike down an act of Parliament as unconstitutional. Judges have recently become more active in reviewing the actions of government but, with the one glaring exception of European law, this judicial oversight has been mostly confined to deciding whether individual ministers have been acting within existing laws and guidelines set by Parliament (that is, the government itself or its predecessors). This can be bothersome to ministers but, if they feel too bothered by a specific judicial ruling, they can simply pass another law making their actions legal, even retrospectively.

Ironically, parliamentary sovereignty seemed too extreme a proposition even for Dicey, its greatest champion. A committed unionist, he was appalled at Gladstone's policy of Irish Home Rule and complained, quite correctly, that it was a fundamental constitutional change. But his doctrine of parliamentary sovereignty left no distinction between constitutional changes and trivial changes to the Highway Code (there is still no such distinction today). So Dicey, remarkably, became the first to advocate the referendum in Britain as 'the one available check on the recklessness of party leaders'.

Later, in 1913, he also argued that, if Parliament passed Asquith's Irish Home Rule Bill, it would not be valid, and that Ulster unionists should resort to rebellion to stop it being implemented. So much for the absolute sovereignty of Parliament and the rule of law. Dicey failed to get his referendum and Ireland was later partitioned after rebellion by Irish nationalists and threats of rebellion by Ulster unionists. National referendums have been advocated occasionally since Dicey's day (mostly by Conservatives opposed to proposed changes), but Britain did not get one until Labour's referendum on membership of the European Community in 1975.

So the traditionalist's view, at least as stated here, rests on a mixture of misconception and complacency. Misconception, because it fails to note that concern about the lack of checks in the British system have been held by some of the heroes of the traditionalist cause. But complacency because it fails to see that over time the basis of its own case has been undermined.

There is another way in which to state the traditionalist case. This was featured in Friedrich Hayek's *The Road to Serfdom*, the great Austrian economist's statement of the case for liberalism and against collectivism. Hayek outlined the importance of the rule of law in a democratic constitution, which is that it provides perceptible limits to the government's coercive power, and thus makes governmental behaviour more or less predictable. This provides individuals with the freedom to organize their own affairs safe in the knowledge that government will not be able to act in an arbitrary and discriminatory way, and with effective means of redress if it does.

Hayek claimed that although this rule of law is normally provided by a Bill of Rights or a Constitutional Code, in Britain it has been provided by firmly established tradition rather than written codes. Adherence to those traditions has had the same effect as would written rules. Hayek may have been writing somewhat too kindly of Britain because he was sitting in the London School of Economics and focusing his attention on Germany and Russia. Nevertheless this view has been echoed by other commentators, such as Professor Peter Hennessy of the University of London, who attribute the British system to the 'good chap theory of government'. In other words, civil servants and politicians have been reliably good chaps, coming from 'sound' social and educational backgrounds and with shared values, ensuring that there really has been nothing to worry about.

The trouble with this view is, first, that it was always somewhat misleading: traditions have frequently been a disguise for abrupt changes and even somewhat arbitrary actions. But even if it were once true it is now impossibly out of date. Britain is no longer run by a small club of good chaps; just as the City of London was forced to modernize and cease to rely on clubbish rules, so British government is going to have to accept that the clubbish era is over. Most of all, faith in the rule of law has been damagingly eroded: the ideas that justice is blind, that bureaucrats are impartial, that liberties are thoroughly protected are all under threat.

Use and Abuse

Parliament is sovereign, but weak. The party system, first past the post elections and efficient party discipline give the government of the day immense power. That power is in turn shared only with the Civil Service and with any governmental agencies responsible to it. There are no effective checks on the power of the government beyond the general election, and thus public opinion expressed through the press. The judiciary acts as only a loose check, ruling only on whether the government is obeying existing laws, but subject always to the blunt truth that the government is capable of changing those laws virtually at will.

What is more, this concentration of power in the cabinet has usually rested on a tenuous democratic mandate. No party since 1935 has won more than 50 per cent of the votes cast. Their minority victories have not stopped both Tory and Labour governments from claiming the right to steer the country abruptly in new directions. The Labour government of 1945 launched a massive nationalization programme and created the welfare state after garnering only 48 per cent of the votes cast. In the 1951 election the Labour government lost power to the Tories, a defeat widely seen as a decision by the voters to call a halt to further socialist measures, even though Labour's share of votes cast actually rose to 49 per cent (exceeding that of the victorious Tories by 1 per cent). Mrs (now Lady) Thatcher launched her free-market counterrevolution after winning only 46 per cent of the vote in 1979 and only 42 per cent in her two subsequent elections.

The electoral system has been brutal to third parties, for all practical purposes disenfranchising millions of voters. In the 1983 and 1987 elections the Liberal-SDP Alliance received 25 per cent and 23 per cent of the votes respectively, but only 4 per cent of seats in the Commons. In 1992 the

Liberal Democrats received 17.8 per cent of the votes, more than half of those cast for Labour, but only 3.1 per cent of Commons seats, compared to Labour's 42 per cent.

In this system of 'strong government', cabinet ministers, and the vast government bureaucracy over which they preside, have been the exclusive arbiters of what the public should know. British governments run by both main parties have been among the most secretive of all the Western democracies, refusing to grant the public, from whom they are supposed to derive their legitimacy, any legal rights to information about, or held by, their government. Often the only way British voters discover what the government has really been up to is when ministers leak information to discredit each other, or when a scandal or blunder forces it to divulge information to limit damage to its own political prospects (though even this can backfire, as it seems to have done with the *Scott Report*).

With no Bill of Rights to constrain them, both Labour and Tory governments have extended police powers, restricted press freedom, and suspended the ordinary workings of the criminal law (as they have done for more than twenty years in both Northern Ireland and, through various Prevention of Terrorism Acts, in the rest of Britain). These moves have touched on the basic freedoms of all citizens, but have been impossible to challenge in British courts. Britain has the worst record of any European nation before the European Court of Human Rights.

In 1994 the government virtually abolished the right to silence in criminal trials after little debate in the Commons. The measure is contained in a mere four sections of a giant 169-section statute. Whatever the merits or demerits of this action it did, at a stroke, eliminate a right which had, for centuries, been thought a pillar of Britain's judicial system. This might have deserved a bit more debate, and some reference to the citizens whose rights were being so curtailed.

Explicit constitutional reform to rein in the powers of government may have proved difficult in the past, but the lack of a codified constitution has allowed governments to innovate in ways which, in most other democratic countries, would be deemed constitutional changes, and so subject to special procedures to win the consent of the electorate. Since 1979, for example, the Tories have drastically reduced the powers of local authorities.

And, when it comes to Europe, the enormous discretion in the hands of British governments has led to what can only be described as a constitutional catastrophe. The Tory government which led Britain into the European Community in 1973 explicitly promised in a 1971 white paper that membership presented 'no question of any erosion of essential national sovereignty' and that 'our courts will continue to operate as they do at present'. Any constitutional implications were also played down during

Labour's referendum three years later, and were brushed aside by the Thatcher and Major governments when they signed the Single European Act and the Maastricht Treaty. In fact, membership has blown a hole right through the middle of Dicey's doctrine of parliamentary sovereignty. The Tory Maastricht rebels were correct, at least about this.

Pooling powers with Britain's EU partners may be in Britain's long-term interests. But even an avid pro-European should feel uncomfortable that such a momentous change to the foundations of Britain's system of government was made without consulting the British electorate. France and Germany, like other EU countries, made explicit changes to their written constitutions to endorse the transfer of powers to the EU. Britain seems to have sleepwalked to the same destination. The electorate was never given any real choice in the matter.

Is Reform Possible?

The consequences of this use and abuse of the concentration of power in the cabinet have been enfeebling rather than crippling, but that still makes them serious. The most general consequence of the enfeeblement of the British constitution has been a gradual erosion of support for the political system and of faith both in government and in the judicial system, as the checks on government have been shown to be inadequate.

For this reason there is increasing interest in reform. Campaigning groups such as Charter 88 (membership 55,000) have demonstrated a growing interest in changes to the way Britain is governed. A MORI opinion poll for the Joseph Rowntree Reform Trust, published in May 1995, found 79 per cent of respondents in favour of a written constitution, 79 per cent wanting a Bill of Rights, 81 per cent for a freedom of information act and 77 per cent supporting the more frequent use of referendums.

In principle, that ought to make reform more or less inevitable. But it is not. Reforms have been discussed many times in the past; the problems have appeared just as pressing. Yet nothing has been done.

One basic obstacle to reform is the fact that the most commonly proposed changes are meant to reduce the power of central government, but can be pursued only by the party in power which, naturally, finds this prospect less than appealing. In this century constitutional reform has been, typically, far more attractive to oppositions than to governing parties. The Tories flirted with reform in the 1970s while out of power, when Lord Hailsham famously complained that Britain's constitutional arrangements were moving it towards an 'elective dictatorship'. Ensconced on the Woolsack a few years later as Margaret Thatcher's first Lord Chancellor, his interest in radical reform—and that of most other Tories—evaporated.

If Labour wins the next general election, after nearly two decades in opposition, it could undergo a similar transformation. Sharing or reducing its newly-won power through reform measures—which themselves are bound to be complicated and contentious—could quickly seem to be less urgent than wielding that power to pursue its own policies on education, health, the economy, or foreign affairs. Labour's leaders are already sounding less enthusiastic about some of the party's constitutional promises, and it remains to be seen whether all such promises are included in Labour's election manifesto. It is also far from clear whether the public's low regard for British institutions reflects an appetite for real change or simply disgust at an extremely unpopular Tory government which has been in office for too long. A set of fresh faces at the top may be enough to cheer up most voters, at least initially.

The biggest obstacle to constitutional reform, however, is not the lethargy or self-interest of politicians, but the ingrained conservativism which runs through both main parties and the wider electorate. Most Britons seem wary of rapid change, suspicious of grand schemes of improvement and reluctant to abandon the tried and true for the uncertainties of the new. The case for constitutional reform is a powerful one. But all too often its advocates assume that the need for reform is obvious, and opposition to it merely self-interested.

Traditionalists are right to argue that Britain is not facing war, revolution, or political collapse. But they are wrong to assume that it is only some wrenching crisis which justifies or makes possible constitutional change. Though few democratic nations have faced the kind of top-to-bottom changes now advocated by British reformers, many other countries (Canada, New Zealand, and Australia are recent examples) have made significant constitutional changes without facing such a crisis.

In the end, the case for the introduction of a genuine rule of law, using a Bill of Rights and a constitutional code to define the limits to governmental action, and empowering the judiciary to act as constitutional custodians, must rest on the myriad of grievances and imperfections that have been seen and felt in Britain in the past several decades. Only through such real grievances will popular opinion be marshalled in favour of change.

What is striking, however, is that the principles favouring such reforms now have a firmly multi-party character. The Labour Party has in the past been the most frequent advocate of constitutional reform, partly out of opposition to entrenched privilege (as in the House of Lords) but partly also to paint itself as tribune of the people against the ravages of big government. That desire has foundered not only in Labour's self-interest when in in power but also on a philosophical contradiction: Labour claims to favour freedom but has actually, through its collectivist, big government urges, encouraged coercion.

Tony Blair's leadership of Labour is, however, changing this: although he has shown some interest in a doctrine of communitarianism which is also ultimately coercive, his more basic drift has been towards smaller government, towards individualistic, market-based policies and towards an emphasis on personal freedoms. Mr Blair, if he gets his way, will be closer to a Social Democrat or even a Liberal, than to old Labour.

The Liberal Democratic Party, when it resists big government solutions, has always harboured philosophical leanings appropriate to the dispersal of power and the entrenchment of the rule of law. The big questions, however, lie in the Conservative Party.

For the time being, the Conservatives look ineluctably opposed to constitutional reform. John Major has noisily declared himself against devolution, against the dispersal of power and, in effect, against a Bill of Rights. Even the Tory radicals such as John Redwood and Michael Portillo have declared their love for parliamentary sovereignty and against reform.

Yet these radicals do hold the key to change. For, in the end, radicalism and Toryism are in contradiction to one another. Margaret Thatcher's Toryism was concerned with the destruction of institutions, with reform, and most of all with the shrinking of the state. She and her self-proclaimed heirs claim to favour constitutional tradition. That compromise was founded, ultimately, on the need to maintain solidarity in the Tory party. But, in the end, even politicians find contradictions impossible to maintain. And once the Tories are out of office, those contradictions are likely to break through to the surface.

True Thatcherism, based on the ideas of Keith Joseph, Arthur Seldon, and Friedrich Hayek, should favour the rule of law. Shrinking the state merely by reducing public spending and public ownership ought not to be enough; it can be reversed by subsequent governments. To fulfill the Thatcherite and Hayekian ideal you need permanent restraints of the activities of the state, restraints that subsequent governments will find it very hard, or preferably impossible, to overturn. Only then can the individual really be protected against coercion by the state; only then can the individual safely organize his affairs free of the fear of arbitrary interference.

A certain basic arrogance among Tories has prevented this philosophy from emerging. This arrogance assumes that as long as Tories dominate the government, 'good chaps' will be in charge and the individual will not need to be protected. In opposition, with the prospect quite possibly of a long period out of government, this view could well change. The Tory right will need a new rallying cry. Hostility to Europe will not do. Restraining the state; completing Lady Thatcher's task; entrenching the rule of law: those are the principles that could, nay should, again rally the right.

8

Incorporation and the Loss of Illusions

RICHARD WILMOT-SMITH QC

For those of us who, like me, were born in the ten years after the Second World War, there has been a steady process of disillusionment. However, I use the word disillusion unemotionally without implying either pain or disquiet. As the illusions imparted to us by parents, teachers, and society in general are shown to be false and unreal, so we as individuals must come to deal with the world as it is rather than as we were taught. Probably the most newsworthy source of disillusion shared by us all concerns personal disclosures about the Royal Family. It is easy to understand that those concerned are merely human beings with strengths and weaknesses common to us all. The illusion that royalty are somehow special and demanding of singular deference and respect above and beyond that of ordinary people is, by now, easily and painlessly discarded.

Other illusions are harder to dispose of. On the map of the world a comforting proportion used to be coloured pink and this was as much a source of pride as the defeat of the Spanish Armada. There was no suggestion then that the colonization of India ought truly to have been a source of shame. Now most of us accept that the British Empire was built at the cost of the lives and liberties of people we had no business ruling.

The loss of illusion has coincided with the 'relative decline' of this country as an economic power. Overall we are, at last, coming to accept that we have a lot to learn from other countries whose people use different alphabets and have different coloured skin and whose economic performance is superior to ours.

There has also been a loss of illusion about our system of justice and the judges themselves. It was not that long ago that the Lord Chief Justice was able to pronounce in public upon the universal admiration in which our judges were held. It was accepted that our common law was a unique creation of infinite merit and that our system of justice was the best in the world. It is no longer painful or heretical for lawyers to see those illusions for what they are. Recently most judges would have denied that there was any need for judicial training.[1] Now judicial training is built into our system

---

[1] For a good example of hostility to such a course see Lord Devlin's book *The Judge* (Oxford University Press, 1979), pp. 34–48.

with an active Judicial Studies Board and the only debate on the matter relates to how much more training there should be.

Our judges are subject to an appropriate scepticism about their frailties and competence. However the loss of illusions about our judges is more seriously and lastingly concentrated upon the extraordinary number of miscarriages of justice which have come to light in the last few years. With such a record we can no longer claim to have the best system of justice in the world.

Those of us who practise private law in international arbitrations are only too aware that our civil law is not necessarily the best in the world. Practitioners who go to the Far East and the Middle East become familiar with the fact that for nearly every proposition of English Law there is an equivalent one in the jurisdiction they are visiting. For every way round a problem that the English legal system has, there is an equally efficacious one in the foreign jurisdiction. Those who pronounced that our law was the best in the would were not comparative lawyers, but their view was unchallenged.

With the departure of these illusions, held dear for so long, must come an examination of our constitution and the place of the European Convention on Human Rights in our law.

Parliament and the European Convention

The easy assumption, and source of pride, that our unwritten constitution is the best in the world has long been part of our national consciousness. The time has come when an examination of that assumption is acceptable and necessary. If today you ask the question: 'Should there not be some document which sets out what the rights of our citizens are and what their relationship is to the executive and legislature?' You would inexorably get the answer 'Yes'. A few years ago you might have got the answer 'Yes, for everyone else'. In fact, the European Convention was a British idea put forward for a Europe which had to learn about democracy and freedom in the aftermath of the Second World War. No more can we say that we have nothing to learn on such topics.

We can no longer shelter behind our national conceit, however sophisticated we pretend to be. We must state what values we hold and adhere to those values regardless of day-to-day pressures upon them. The continued refusal to do so is intellectually and morally untenable. This situation is particularly ridiculous given that this country, as one of the 'High Contracting Parties' to the Convention has agreed to it and for thirty years has agreed to honour the various judgments of the European Court of Human

Rights. Since 1966 individuals have had the right to petition the European Commission for Human Rights.[2]

In any civilized society there is a need for majorities to be fettered in their ability to oppress. This is not a recently perceived need. During the debate about the Bill of Rights in the United States, James Madison wrote to Thomas Jefferson on 17 October 1788 as follows:

Wherever the real power in a government lies, there is a danger of oppression. In our governments the real power lies in the majority of the Community, and the invasion of private rights is *chiefly* to be apprehended, not from acts of Government contrary to the sense of its constituents, but from acts which the Government is the mere instrument of the major number of the Constituents. This is a truth of great importance, but not sufficiently attended to; and is probably more strongly impressed on my mind by the facts, and reflections suggested by them, than on yours which has contemplated abuses of power arising from a very different quarter. Wherever there is an interest and power to do wrong, wrong will generally be done, and not less readily by a powerful and interested party than by a powerful and interested prince .

Madison's analysis puts the blame on the majority of people. In our system of government that majority is translated, imperfectly, into a majority on the House of Commons. Therefore in our political debate the complaints of the minorities suffering, as Madison analysed it, are to be found in the complaints of Her Majesties' Opposition of the day.

Political opponents have always decried the illiberality of the party in government. The Tories of the 1960s criticized the Wilson Government for being 'doctrinaire' with just the same zeal as the Major Government is attacked by the Labour Party. Complaints about socialist 'confiscation' match complaints about Conservative insensitivity to the rights of trade unionists and minorities. It goes against the grain for an elected government to enact legislation which prospectively limits its powers or abilities such as, for example, the ability to suppress information available to the electorate. The Conservative Government elected in 1970 promised 'Open Government'. Once in office, nothing changed.

However it is becoming obvious that Parliament has less and less power to control events in the economic sphere,where much of the national debate takes place. The power of the European Commission to touch the lives of all of us is obvious. The fact that a simple repeal of Section 2 of the European Communities Act 1972 would do away with all that does not alter that position. Thoughts of such a repeal do not occupy the mainstream of

---

[2] On 14 January 1966 Harold Wilson's Labour government deposited the appropriate declaration in accordance with Article 25 of the Convention.

our political life and are not seriously debated. There is acceptance of, if not universal agreement with, the concept that a Directive from Brussels will override incompatible domestic legislation.

It is widely believed that the law of the European Union is unaffected by the Convention. However this might well be wrong. On 5 April 1977 the European Parliament, the European Council, and the Commission adopted the following declaration:

1. The European Parliament, the Council and the Commission stress the prime importance they attach to the protection of fundamental rights, as derived in particular form the constitution of the member-states and the European Convention for the Protection of Human Rights and Fundamental Freedoms.
2. In the exercise of their powers and in particular the aims of the European Communities they respect and will continue to respect these rights.[3]

The German Constitutional Court has said on the same topic:

All the main institutions of the Community have since acknowledged in a legally significant manner that in the exercise of their powers and the pursuit of their objectives of the Community they will be guided as a legal duty by respect for fundamental rights, in particular as established by *the constitutions of member states and by the European Convention on Human Rights.*[4]

The words 'in a legally significant manner' and 'guided as a legal duty by respect for fundamental rights', used by a Court of great persuasive weight in considering the 1977 declaration, suggest that the Convention might be invoked with success in our own courts at some future point even without incorporation. However, the case law as it stands at present in this country suggests that this is still some way off.

In economic policy there is a further powerful *de facto* fetter upon Parliament's sovereignty. That is the power of hot money in the now deregulated financial markets. The trend towards powerlessness at Westminster in the face of such financial whirlwinds has been long established. Prime Minister Wilson complained of, and was hostage to, the 'Gnomes of Zurich' thirty years ago. Any government's interest rate policy, and therefore economic policy, is now circumscribed by what the markets will allow, as 'Black Wednesday' attests.

Therefore Parliamentary sovereignty is theoretical. Limits upon what Parliament can control are there either as a result of enactment by Parliament itself or as a result of events.

---

[3] [1977] OJ C103/1.
[4] The Court's italics. *Re the Application of Wunsche Handelgesellschaft* [1987] 3 CMLR 225 at 259.

The House of Lords Select Committee Report

The reaction to power, *de facto* or *de jure*, slipping away from Westminster might be to try to ensure that no more leaves and refuse to incorporate. However the arguments against incorporation are threadbare and have been exposed somewhat mercilessly by other writers. I shall deal only with six particular arguments which appeared in the Report of the Select Committee of the House of Lords on a Bill of Rights[5] as being reasons why there should not be incorporation and have not been specifically addressed by other writers in this book.

The first was that incorporation would 'graft on to the existing law and Act of Parliament in a form totally at variance with any existing legislation and indeed incompatible with such legislation.' It went on

Incorporation of the Convention would, for the first time, open up wide areas in which legislative policy on such matters as race relations, freedom of speech, freedom of the press, privacy, education and forms of punishment would be effectively handed over to the judiciary. All these are matters which our constitution has hitherto reposed in the legislature.

The argument relating to form is simply wrong. There have been many legislative enactments of treaty obligations in both public[6] and private[7] law.

The suggestion that the obligations contained in the Convention are at variance with existing legislation is something no government dare admit today because that would involve an admission that the United Kingdom is in default of its treaty obligations. In March 1978 the last Labour Government stated in a written answer 'The Government have at present no reason to suppose that there is a conflict between any of the provisions of the Convention and the law of the United Kingdom or the general rules governing administrative practice in this country . . .' The present government's current position can be expected to be no different.

The statement that there will be whole swathes of legislative policy handed over to the judges implies that existing legislation, as enacted, and the common law, as laid down, are contrary to the Convention. Were it otherwise, there would be nothing to fear. However nobody today would suggest that was the case.

Nevertheless there is a serious point that cannot be ignored, namely that the courts will have the power to declare legislation to be incompatible with the Convention and therefore illegal or unenforceable. This power already exists in relation to the laws of the European Union. Therefore nothing new would be added to our unwritten constitution by incorporation.

[5] HL 176, 1977–8, 30–34.
[6] The Maastricht Treaty's incorporation is the most recent example.
[7] E.g., The Civil Jurisdiction and Judgments Act 1982.

Nevertheless the incorporation of the Convention would be a significant extension of the power. Other countries have come to see the logical consequence which flows from this, namely the creation of a constitutional court. Germany established theirs in 1951, Italy in 1953, France in 1958, and Spain in 1980. The establishment of such a court in this Country would allow a fresh look at the method of appointing the judges and their tenure so as to draw the sting of the 'unelected' and 'unrepresentative' charge now made against our judiciary. A court with a fixed number that sits together all the time, and does not break down into committees appointed behind closed doors, would acquire a recognizable character. Its legitimacy could be reinforced by an appropriately open procedure of appointment where the views of prospective appointees could be examined.

The second objection raised by the Select Committee was that the courts would have to change from their case-by-case approach. The Committee puts it that

Under the common law the courts have developed legal principles slowly and empirically, from case to case. Under a Bill of Rights they would start with principles of the widest generality and would have a free hand to decide how those principles operated in the cases that came before them.

This objection has a somewhat naïve view of the common law, which can turn on a sixpence if policy drives the judges to it.[8] Common law jurisdictions can and do operate under a Bill of Rights, the United States is the oldest example, but the recent New Zealand and Canadian experience does not demonstrate that the common law approach is destroyed by the single enactment of a Bill of Rights. To say that judges have a 'free hand' puts forward the proposition that the judges would not be fettered by the words of the Convention and have to operate it within the corpus of law laid down by the European Court of Human Rights. Judges have to interpret the law of the European Union today without being in possession of a 'free hand'. There is no reason why the interpretation of the Convention should be any different.

The third objection is a variation on the other two, namely that Parliament is ready to interfere in new areas where problems have arisen and

it is better for Parliament to enact detailed legislation . . . rather than to look to the unelected judges to develop both the policy on such matters and the way in which it should be dealt with . . .

Naturally if Parliament has enacted detailed legislation in accordance with the Convention, then there is no scope for judicial intervention. If, however, Parliament has not done so, then the citizens of this country are for practical

---

[8] For a good example in the area involving the private law obligations of local authorities see *Anns* v. *Merton* [1978] AC 728 and *Murphy* v. *Brentwood District Council* [1991] 1 AC 398.

purposes without the protection of basic rights which this country says it is obliged to provide as a treaty obligation. It is when Parliament does not act that the Convention is needed.

The fourth objection is that the law should be clear and certain and incorporation would

introduce a substantial and wide ranging element of uncertainty into our law . . . To take only one example, the introduction of Article 10 of the European Convention into our domestic law would introduce serious doubts into such important areas of the law as those relating to defamation and contempt of court and official secrets.

This objection adheres to some of the conceits to which I have referred earlier. The suggestion is that other jurisdictions have a system of law which is more uncertain than ours and therefore their jurisprudence suffers less from the injection of the Convention into their system of law than ours would. It would be a brave comparative lawyer who seriously suggested that certainty in the law was less prized across the English Channel. It must be accepted, however, that some uncertainty will attend the immediate aftermath of incorporation. But that uncertainty only arises from the need for the courts to establish whether our law actually complies with our treaty obligations.

The fifth objection is that the Convention

would have a life of its own quite independent of its international existence. The Convention could then be invoked daily in our Courts and they would constantly have to give decisions on it without any guidance from jurisprudence at Strasbourg. Moreover our Courts would be free to give the Convention a wider effect than required by such Strasbourg jurisprudence as was available.

To object to the incorporation of the Convention on the ground that it would be used in our domestic courts has little intellectual and moral merit. The statement that the Convention would have a 'life of its own' is not well founded. Courts could not depart from the principles set out in the Convention and the decisions of the European Court of Human Rights.

The sixth objection is that 'The present situation in the United Kingdom is in accord with the original philosophy of the European Convention'. In support of this view was the statement that 'it is not the case, as some of the witnesses assumed, that relatively more cases have gone to the Commission from the United Kingdom than from other countries'.

If the position really is that the present state of the law and administrative practice is in accord with the Convention, it is difficult to see what harm comes from incorporation other than to take up parliamentary time. Equally there cannot be many cases where the Convention is subject to contention in our courts because our law complies. However the position is unambiguously the opposite and that is why the United Kingdom has such a poor record before the Court.

Conclusion

It would weary the reader if I went on to consider the other and less cogent arguments. Fresh arguments have been raised by opponents and are covered by other contributors. Their fallaciousness can almost be touched. One is driven to the conclusion that there is a combination of two factors at work. Firstly the acceptance of the arguments is borne of beliefs not open to question. The process of disillusion, to which I refer above, has not begun. Secondly simple *realpolitik* demands that the party in office would like to do as it wishes. Therefore, as an example, Lord Hailsham can complain in opposition about an 'elective dictatorship' but then belong to a government which does not introduce a Bill of Rights.

A citizen can draw a number of uncharitable conclusions about how this situation has been allowed to continue. The delay and expense of going to Europe must be considered a useful countervailing force to the formal embrace which this country gives to the Convention. We can say we endorse the Convention but at the same time ensure that it is invoked as little as possible. The fewer cases that finally get to the court, it must be thought, the better. Successive governments have made it clear that they would find actual and automatic compliance with the Convention irksome. The present government's reaction to the Gibraltar killings case was hysterical and ill judged, but perhaps embodies the typical reaction of a guilty executive which would rather do without the rights to which they formally subscribe. Past Labour governments have been equally hostile because they have seen the Convention as a fetter upon their ambitions of social engineering. It will be interesting to see if the Labour Party, once in office, fulfils its pledge to incorporate.

9

Taking Human Rights Seriously[1]

LORD LESTER QC[2]

I have chosen as my title 'Taking Human Rights Seriously', not because I, an utter barrister, would be so foolish as to attempt an analysis of Professor Ronald Dworkin's principles of jurisprudence, but because I want to consider how seriously Parliament, Government, and the courts take the international human rights codes by which they are bound internationally but not yet by domestic law. What I say will be critical of the failure of successive governments to take human rights sufficiently seriously at home in this country, of a lack of openness and candour by Ministers and civil servants about compliance with international human rights treaty obligations, and about the lack of effective Parliamentary scrutiny of what has been happening. I should, however, like to say that some of my best friends are civil servants, that I greatly respect their professional skill, if not their obsessive secrecy, and that I especially admire the work done by Baroness Chalker and her Human Rights Unit within the Foreign and Commonwealth Office. They cannot fairly be criticized for a failure to take the effective protection of human rights sufficiently seriously.

The Failure to Incorporate the European Convention

A decade ago, in another public lecture,[3] I recalled the Attlee Government's dislike of the European Convention on Human Rights (a sentiment doubtless privately shared by the Major Government with as much passionate intensity). I shall briefly do so again because the story remains instructive.

Lord Chancellor Jowitt was troubled that the Convention would prevent a future British Government from detaining people without trial during a period of emergency (under the notorious Regulation 18 (b)); or judges from sending litigants to prison for throwing eggs at them; or the Home

---

[1] Text of the Paul Sieghart Memorial Lecture 1994 delivered to the British Institute of Human Rights at King's College London.

[2] Lord Lester of Herne Hill is a Liberal Democrat peer and a constitutional lawyer.

[3] 'Fundamental Rights: The United Kingdom Isolated?'. *Public Law*, Spring 1984.

Secretary from banning Communist or Fascist demonstrations. Chancellor of the Exchequer Stafford Cripps instructed the Cabinet that a government committed to a planned economy could not ratify the Convention because it would prevent his inspectors from using their wide powers to enter people's homes. Colonial Secretary Jim Griffiths, a latter-day Lord North, feared that 'extremist politicians' would exploit the Convention in the colonies, the bulk of whose people were 'still politically immature'. The Lord Chancellor, having criticized the loose drafting of the Convention (by senior British lawyers) and the ways in which it might alter our common law and statute law, complained that the Convention would 'jeopardise our whole system of law', and upset our senior judges.

The Attlee Government was firmly opposed not only to the Convention but also to the so-called 'right of petition' or complaint to the European Commission of Human Rights, and to the powers of the European Court of Human Rights (the ECHR). Eventually and with much private grumbling, the Attlee Government were driven by their political isolation in Europe to ratify the Convention. But they resolved never to allow British citizens to invoke its guarantees against them in Strasbourg.

The Attlee Government's decision to ratify the Convention was taken without any Parliamentary approval or even debate—as was the decision by the second Wilson Government in 1976 to become bound by the International Covenant on Civil and Political Rights. So too was the most momentous decision of all, by the first Wilson Government in December 1965: to allow us, the people, to take to the European Commission and Court of Human Rights our complaints of breaches of human rights by Parliament, Government, or the courts. By that decision, a large slice of sovereign power passed from Westminster and Whitehall to Strasbourg. Yet not even a Cabinet Committee—still less Parliament—was consulted about this radical change in government policy and constitutional practice. It was decided by Ministers in interdepartmental correspondence,[4] and Parliament was informed only after the decision had been taken.[5]

For almost half a century, successive governments and senior civil servants have firmly opposed every attempt to make international human rights law directly enforceable in our courts. When I worked as Roy Jenkins' special adviser, in the mid-1970s, there was a concerted effort by Ministers and mandarins to prevent us from publishing a muted Green Paper on incorporation of the Convention—an issue considered to be likely to give the politically immature people of this country dangerously radical ideas.

---

[4] 'Fundamental Rights: The United Kingdom Isolated?'. *Public Law*, Spring 1984, pp. 58–61.

[5] Hansard (HC), Vol. 722, col. 235, 7 Dec. 1965.

A key question was glossed over in that obscurely published and little noticed discussion paper of ours. The question is whether it is compatible with the law of the Constitution of Parliament to continue to fail to incorporate the European Convention (and the International Covenant) into our domestic law. How does that continuing failure square with the basic doctrine of parliamentary sovereignty—that it is for Parliament, rather than for the executive or the judges, to make the law?

As every schoolgirl knows, the doctrine of parliamentary sovereignty springs from the 'glorious bloodless' Revolution of 1688–9, reinforced by the theories of Jeremy Bentham and his disciples. It teaches that it is for the people's elected representatives to 'make the law'; that judges lack the necessary domestic mandate or skills to act as lawmakers; that American or French revolutionary talk of fundamental—or 'natural and imprescriptible—rights, is 'nonsense on stilts'; and that our omnipotent Parliament is the main protector of our rights.

As every constitutional lawyer knows,[6] Parliamentary sovereignty requires that, while ministers may freely make treaties, and enter into binding international obligations, ministers must seek parliamentary approval where the existing law is affected, or where our private rights are interfered with by a treaty, or where a grant from public funds is made necessary. That is why Parliament enacted the European Communities Act 1972—to give domestic effect to the Treaty of Rome.

Lord Chancellor Jowitt was a good enough constitutional lawyer to know that when the Government ratified the European Convention it would be necessary (in the words of his memorandum of October 1950 to the Cabinet) 'to bring in legislation applying the conditions of the Convention to our domestic law'. For this was unlike any previous treaty ratified by any British Government. It obliged the States Parties to secure those human rights and freedoms to everyone within their jurisdiction, and to provide effective national remedies for violations of its terms; and it conferred enforceable rights upon individuals against the public authorities of their own States.

So it was obvious to Lord Chancellor Jowitt, when he wrote his memorandum to the Cabinet, in October 1950, that ratification of the Convention would affect existing law and private rights in this country, and that Parliament would therefore need to legislate to give domestic effect to its provisions. On 4 November 1950, the Convention was signed in Rome. Under

---

[6] Where taxation is imposed or a grant from public funds rendered necessary, or where the existing law is affected, as in the case of multi-national conventions, or where the private rights of the subject are interfered with by a treaty . . . the previous or subsequent consent of Parliament is in all cases required to render the treaty binding upon the subject and enforceable by officers of the Crown. *Halsbury's Laws* (4th ed.) Vol.8, para. 986. See also the cases there referred to.

the so-called 'Ponsonby Rule',[7] the Convention was laid on the table of both Houses of Parliament for a period of twenty-one days. The Ponsonby Rule also requires that,

In the case of important treaties, the Government will, of course, take an opportunity of submitting them to the House for discussion within this period . . . His Majesty's Government desire that Parliament should . . . exercise supervision over agreements . . . by which the nation may be bound in certain circumstances.

In this respect the Ponsonby Rule was breached, or else the Convention was not considered to be a sufficiently important treaty to be submitted to Parliament for discussion.

On 13 November 1950, during a debate to take note of the deliberations in the Council of Europe, Foreign Secretary Ernest Bevin, who together with Kenneth Younger, had conducted the negotiations on the Convention, explained[8] to the Commons that the Convention 'has to be woven into our law'. Both the Foreign Secretary, publicly, and the Lord Chancellor, privately, expected that Parliament would be asked to weave the fabric of the Convention into domestic law: that is to enact legislation. Yet only a week later, the Attorney-General, Sir Hartley Shawcross, told[9] the Commons, that it was 'not contemplated that any legislation will be necessary in order to give effect to the terms of this Convention'. Sir H. Williams MP then asked, 'Are we to understand that the Charter has made really no difference so far as this country is concerned?' The Attorney-General replied: 'I think we are entitled to say that the law of this country has always been in advance of the laws of most other countries in regard to human rights.' Mr Boyd-Carpenter MP asked Shawcross: 'Do the Government now intend to withdraw Defence Regulation 58A'; but, happily for the Government, there was no time left for an answer.

The United Kingdom was the first country to ratify the Convention, on 8 March 1951. Successive governments ever since have side-stepped the question as to whether legislation is necessary to give it domestic effect. They have done so by arguing that our law adequately matches Convention law without the need for legislative action. Until United Kingdom acceptance of the right of petition in 1966 they were able to distance themselves from the Convention, and no-one noticed that there was any constitutional problem. Since 1966, they have continued to argue that our law mirrors and reflects Convention law; except, that is, where the ECHR (or Whitehall) otherwise decides. When that happens the Government asks Parliament to legislate (for example, on contempt of court, or corporal punishment in

[7] See generally, Report of the House of Lords Select Committee on the European Communities on *Political Union: Law-Making Powers and Procedures*, 21 July 1991 (HJ Roper 80) App. 4, para. 4.

[8] Hansard (HC), Vol. 480, col. 1503, 13 Nov. 1950.

[9] Hansard (HC), Vol. 481, 20 Nov. 1950, oral answer, col. 15.

schools, or the powers of the security services), or The Government changes an offending administrative practice (for example, discriminatory immigration controls over British Asian passport holders from East Africa).

When I recently asked whether ratification of the Convention or the Covenant has affected either existing law or the private rights of individuals or corporations in this country, I was not given a direct answer. What I was told by the Government instead[10] was that they 'take full account of their obligations' under those instruments, and that where the United Kingdom 'has been found by the European Court of Human Rights to be in violation of the Convention, it gives effect to those judgments, by amendment to the law or changes in administrative practice, as necessary'.

The official line turns a blind eye to the constitutional significance of what happens when our own courts, understandably restive at having their decisions reviewed by the European Commission and Court of Human Rights in Strasbourg, without being empowered by Parliament to give direct effect to the Convention at home, use the Convention to interpret ambiguous statutes or to develop the common law. This is a most welcome approach by our enlightened senior judiciary because it reduces avoidable inconsistencies between our law and Convention law. But now that our courts use the Convention strongly in this way, the Government cannot credibly maintain the traditional line that ratification does not affect either existing law or private rights in this country, and so does not require an Act of Parliament to give domestic effect to the Convention.

For example, in 1992 the Court of Appeal debarred[11] the Derbyshire County Council from suing the *Sunday Times* for a libel on the council's 'governing reputation'. The decision was based on the need to avoid an unnecessary interference with free speech, in breach of Article 10 of the Convention. The Law Lords upheld the decision[12] without needing to rely upon the Convention, by ruling that the common law matched Article 10. In this case and previous free speech cases (like *Spycatcher*[13]), United Kingdom ratification of the Convention has undoubtably affected existing law and private rights whether by means of judicial interpretation or judicial law-making. I cheer these decisions (as a citizen as well as a professionally-interested advocate); but they show a pressing constitutional need for Parliament to use its much vaunted sovereignty to legitimize what the judges are doing without parliamentary authority.

---

[10] Hansard (HC), Vol. 552, 28 February 1994, W.A. 66.
[11] *Times Newspapers* v. *Derbyshire C.C.* [1992] QB 770.
[12] *Derbyshire C.C.* v. *Times Newspapers* [1993] AC 534.
[13] *A.-G.* v. *Guardian Newspapers Ltd.* [1987] 1 WLR 1248 (HL); *A.-G.* v. *Guardian Newspapers (No. 2)* [1990] 1 AC 109 (HL); *A.-G.* v. *Newspapers Publishing Plc* (CA), 27 Feb. 1990 (unreported).

Incidentally, it seems to me to be strongly arguable that it is constitution-ally and legally necessary to enact legislation to give clear legal authority for paying out of public funds costs that result from the United Kingdom's ratification of the European Convention and from United Kingdom accept-ance of the right of individual petition: to satisfy judgments of the ECHR; to pay the costs of friendly settlements; and to pay contributions towards the cost of the Court and the Commission, and towards the costs of legal aid. I am not an expert in Parliamentary control of public expenditure, but it seems to me that such legislation would give proper effect to the impor-tant constitutional legal requirement that clear statutory authority is needed for public expenditure.[14] I recently asked the Government what is the legal authority for paying out of public funds Strasbourg costs of this kind. Their reply was that[15] 'The United Kingdom is legally bound to meet these costs as a consequence of our ratification of the European Convention . . . The costs are met from the Votes of the Government Departments concerned, as approved by Parliament in the annual Appropriation Act.' I hope that they are right, because otherwise their payments are *ultra vires*. It is not self-evident to me that this constitutes sufficiently clear and specific legislative authority for costs of a recurring nature, so as to pass muster under the special constitutional convention which, in Lord Bridge's words, 'jealously safeguards the exclusive control exercised by parliament over both the levying and the expenditure of public revenue'. That is a further reason why Parliament should give legal effect to the Convention.

Naturally, Whitehall would not be amused by the prospect of legislation to give domestic effect to the Convention. The strength of the continuing opposition within the home Departments should not be underestimated. It led to a clumsy attempt in 1977 to dissuade the Standing Advisory Commis-sion on Human Rights in Northern Ireland from recommending the statu-tory incorporation of the Convention;[16] and an attempt by a senior official to alter what he regarded as the excessively reform-minded composition of an Anglo-American private conference on the same subject in 1984.

It suits the convenience of public officers of the State if those subject to their powers cannot invoke the Convention in British courts to control breaches of human rights. But it is not in the best interests of the people, on whose behalf they exercise their public powers, to be denied speedy and effective remedies in British courts. It makes on sense that—post-*Spycatcher*—our courts, as public authorities bound by the Convention on the international plane, rightly limit their discretionary *judicial* powers to grant injunctions to restrain freedom of expression, or to impose penalties

---

[14] *Holden & Co* v. *C.P.S. (No. 2)* [1993] 2 WLR 934 (HL) at p. 940 *per* Lord Bridge.

[15] Hansard (HL) Vol. 552, 3 Mar. 1994, W.A. 83–4.

[16] The attempt failed. See the Report of the Standing Advisory Committee on Human Rights, *The protection of human rights by law in Northern Ireland.* Cmnd. 7009, Nov. 1977.

for common law contempt of court, because of the Convention; but that—absent Parliamentary authority—they cannot limit the Home Secretary's *administrative* discretion to interfere with broadcasters' free expression in breach of the Convention. It makes no sense that our courts prevent our legislators or administrators from acting expressively or disproportionately in breach of European Community Law,[17] but not to prevent them from acting in breach of European Convention law.

One illustration may serve for all. Marguerite Johnston[18] was a member of the Royal Ulster Constabulary full-time Reserve. The Chief Constable decided not to renew her contract or the contracts of the other women full-time Reservists, nor to give them training in the use of firearms. They brought proceedings against the Chief Constable alleging unlawful sex discrimination. The Secretary of State issued a certificate asserting that what had been done by the Chief Constable had been done for the purpose of safeguarding national security or of protecting public safety or public order. Under domestic law[19] that certificate, unlike a public interest immunity certificate, is deemed to be conclusive evidence that the act complained of was done for that purpose. So Marguerite Johnston and her colleagues were barred by Ministerial fiat from their right of access to the courts, guaranteed by Article 6 of the Convention. Since the Convention is not part of our law, they could not rely on its provisions to overcome the Secretary of State's certificate. But they could rely upon the principle of effective judicial control, laid down in the EEC Council Directive on equal treatment in employment,[20] since Parliament has incorporated that branch of European law into domestic law. So Mrs Johnston took her case before the European Court of Justice (the ECJ), which decided that the principle of effective judicial control did not allow the Secretary of State to prevent her from having the merits of her claim decided by an industrial tribunal in Belfast. In reaching that conclusion, the ECJ observed that the requirement of judicial controls reflects a general principle of law which underlies the constitutional traditions common to the Member States, and which is also laid down in Articles 6 and 13 of the European Convention. The ECJ stated that the principles on which the Convention is based 'must be taken into consideration in Community law'.

Let us suppose that, instead of being the victim of sex discrimination, Mrs Johnston had been the victim of religious or racial discrimination and had brought that complaint in an industrial tribunal. Suppose also that the

[17] See, e.g., *R.* v. *Secretary of State for Employment*, ex p. *EOC* v. [1994] 1 All ER 910.

[18] Case 222/84, *Johnston* v. *Chief Constable of the R.U.C.* [1987] QB 129 (ECJ).

[19] Art. 53(2) of the Sex Discrimination (Northern Ireland) Order 1976 (S.I. 1976 No. 1042 (N.I. 15)).

[20] Art. 6 of Council Dir. No. 76/207/EEC of 9 Feb. 1976 on the implementation of the principle of equal treatment of men and women as regards access to employment, vocational training and promotion and working conditions.

Secretary of State, exercising the equivalent powers conferred upon him in Northern Ireland in relation to complaints of religious discrimination,[21] or upon him in Great Britain in relation to complaints of racial discrimination,[22] then issued a similar certificate depriving her of her right of access to a judicial determination of her complaint. Unless she could prove that the Secretary of State had acted for an improper purpose or had taken leave of his senses in issuing the certificate, she would be unable to review the legality or rationality of the certificate. English judicial review still does not squarely recognize the excessive or disproportionate exercise of a lawful power as an independent ground for judicial review—although there are happy hints of springtime blossom in recent judgments by Mr Justice Laws[23] and Mr Justice Sedley,[24] and even higher.[25] She could not invoke Community law because it does not forbid religious or racial discrimination. Nor, if *Brind*[26] was correctly decided, could she invoke her right of access to the courts, internationally guaranteed by Article 6 of the Convention, as limiting the blanket powers conferred upon the Secretary of State by a docile Parliament. All that she could do would be to take the long and expensive road to the ECHR, seeking a remedy so delayed as to amount to a denial of justice.

It is convenient for administrators that this lamentable situation should continue, but I repeat that it is not in the interests of the citizens of this country, nor is it in the wider public interest.

The European Court of Human Rights—weary of having to decide British cases which could and should have been speedily remedied by British courts—may eventually require the United Kingdom, as it has already required some other Member States, such as Sweden and The Netherlands, to allow more effective judicial review in this country of breaches of human rights. But it would surely be much healthier for our democracy, if Parliament were at last to legislate to secure compliance with British constitutional principles of parliamentary supremacy and the rule of law, rather than in obedience to the judgment of an international court, however distinguished. Parliament could readily command our courts to give the same effect to European Convention law as is given to European Community law, under the European Communities Act. Until it does so, the notion that Parliament takes seriously our internationally guaranteed human

---

[21] S. 42 of the Fair Employment (Northern Ireland) Act 1976 as amended.
[22] Under ss. 41 and 69(2) of the Race Relations Act 1976.
[23] *R.* v. *Somerset C.C.*, ex p. *Fewings, The Times*, 9 Feb. 1994.
[24] *R.* v. *Criminal Injuries Compensation Board*, ex p. *Gambles*, 3 Dec. 1983.
[25] *R.* v. *Independent Television Commission*, ex p. *TSW Broadcasting Ltd* (HL), 26 Mar. 1992 (unreported).
[26] *R.* v. *Secretary of State for the Home Office*, ex p. *Brind* [1991] AC 696 (HL); see the Hon. Sir John Laws, 'Is the High Court the Guardian of Fundamental Constitutional Rights?' [1993] *Public Law* 59.

rights is a nonsense; and effective parliamentary sovereignty is nonsense on stilts.

It follows from the fact that the Convention is not part of our law that members of the public service are under no legally binding duty to comply with its terms. Their obligations—like those of Parliament and the judiciary—are binding only in international law. Those obligations include important reporting requirements upon United Kingdom compliance with the European Convention, the International Covenant, and the various other international human rights treaties to which The United Kingdom is party.

The 1976 Green Paper on incorporation referred, without irony, to Parliament as being 'omnicompetent', and to its role as being 'all-pervasive potentially at least'. What happens in the real world is that Parliament plays scarcely any role. There is no Select Committee of either House to scrutinize whether proposed British legislation is compatible with the international human rights codes. Parliament has no right of access to the Law Officers' opinions on this or indeed any subject. Nor does Parliament see or debate government reports to the Human Rights Committee under the International Covenant, or government reports to specialized human rights monitoring bodies, such as CEDAW (the Committee on the Elimination of Discrimination against Women), CERD (the Committee on the Elimination of Racial Discrimination), and the International Labors Organization (ILO) Committee of Experts.

In order to be prepared for this I decided to carry out a spot check into how these reporting obligations are being carried out by the Government, looking at areas of particular interest to me: sex discrimination, equal pay, and racial discrimination. My research staff, to whom I am greatly indebted, worked heroically to obtain copies of the relevant government reports. They discovered that, apart from the first report to the UN Committee on the Rights of the Child, these reports are not published by HMSO; nor are they routinely placed in the Library of either House. The Commission for Racial Equality has never been consulted about the contents of the twelve government reports to CERD, and does not possess a complete set of them. Odd copies can be obtained from particular NGOs as a kind of samizdat. Eventually, I was able to obtain a copy of the twelfth report to CERD from the Home Office. The other eleven reports are being kept in a depot in Hayes. So I abandoned my check on the standard of government reporting on race discrimination to CERD, and have concentrated instead on the two government reports to CEDAW.

The first substantive report was made in May 1987, six years after the United Kingdom had ratified the Convention on the Elimination of all Forms of Discrimination against Women, with sweeping and unnecessary reservations. The report is 187 pages long. It contains material about all manner of subjects. It explains to CEDAW, for example, that Britain's area is about the same size as Uganda, that its seas are shallow, that it has a generally mild and temperate climate.

The prevailing winds are south westerly and the weather from day to day is mainly influenced by depressions moving eastwards across the Atlantic. The weather is subject to frequent changes but to few extremes of temperature.

The report describes the weather at considerably greater lengths, takes the reader on a ramble across the mountains and valleys of the entire British Isles, and discusses social trends, such as the fact that 'Watching television is the main evening activity for all except young men'. The section on Parliament explains to the foreign reader that it is the supreme legislative authority.

Free from any legal restraints imposed by a written constitution Parliament is able to legislate as it pleases.

What the report omits to say is that Parliament has not been consulted by the Government, that Parliament has not considered or authorized the report, and that Parliament has no idea of what is being reported to CEDAW. Nor does the report indicate any dissatisfaction within this country with the operation of the sex discrimination and equal pay legislation, whether from the Equal Opportunities Commissions (EOC) for Great Britain and Northern Ireland, or from the courts, or from trade unions and women's organizations.

The Government's second substantive report to CEDAW was published by the Foreign and Commonwealth Office in May 1991. It is 146 pages long, together with fifteen annexes, including a report on a CEDAW feedback seminar in May 1990. When the report was considered by CEDAW in January 1993,[27] the Committee observed that it contained a wealth of valuable information, 'but it could have been more analytical and could have included the most up-to-date information'. Seven pages of the Government's report blandly describe the working of the equal pay and sex discrimination legislation, and the report mentions that the EOC for Great Britain and the EOC for Northern Ireland had made proposals for strengthening the legislation. Neither in the lengthy report nor in any of the annexes is there any mention of what those proposals are, or of the strong criticisms of the uniquely tortuous and complex equal value procedures made by the two EOCs,[28] as well as by senior members of the judiciary, and by Parlia-

[27] Report of the Committee on the Elimination of Discrimination against Women (Twelfth Session), A/48/38, 28 May 1993.

[28] The Government says that the EOC's proposals are not relevant in the context of the reports, but they are including the CRE's proposals in their next report to the Human Rights Committee, Hansard (HL) Vol. 553, 11 April 1994, W.A. 75–6, Hansard (HL), Vol. 553, 12 April 1994, W.A. 88–9.

mentarians; nor is there mention of the dismantling of the collective machinery for securing equal pay, notably, the Central Arbitration Committee and Wages Councils, nor is there mention of the various domestic and European proceedings in which the Government have advocated a narrowly restrictive interpretation of the concepts of equal treatment and equal pay without sex discrimination.

During the very illuminating exchanges between the Head of the Civil Services, Sir Robin Butler, and Presily Baxendale QC, Counsel to Lord Justice Scott's inquiry, Sir Robin was asked about civil service standards in answering parliamentary questions. His statement explained that 'The Government should always give as full information to Parliament as is possible and should take care, save in the most exceptional cases, not to give a false or misleading answer'. I am sure that Sir Robin and his colleagues would accept that the same high standard of disclosure should apply to government reporting to CEDAW and the other international bodies, in accordance with the United Kingdom's international obligations.

These two reports to CEDAW give only half the picture—the part which shows the United Kingdom compliance in a favourable light. If CEDAW's attention had been drawn to the other more negative half of the picture, they would have been much more vigorous in their questioning of the government's representative. I say this with some confidence because I note that the ILO Committee of Experts, which is better informed about these matters, has been much better focused in its dealings with the Government on the subject of equal pay and the United Kingdom's obligations under ILO Convention No. 100, and much more specific and demanding in its requests for relevant information.

It would be naïve to expect complete candour and openness in the Government's reporting to these bodies. Ministers and their advisers regard themselves as in a similarly adversarial relationship to the international human rights bodies as they do to Parliament. In the knowing words of Mr William Waldegrave,[29] who occupied the Orwellian office of Minister for Open Government, 'Much of government activity is much more like playing poker than playing chess. You don't put all your cards up at one time'. I agree with Mr Waldegrave about this and disagree with his critics who seem to regard the relationship between Government and Parliament as if the Government were responding as a witness on oath in a court of law. Under our system of government, civil servants serve the interests of their ministers, who naturally volunteer as little politically embarrassing information to their Parliamentary critics as they can. There is nothing new or surprising about this. With the experience of the wartime

---

[29] See, e.g., *The Times*, 9 March 1994.

coalition government, and the Attlee Government, George Orwell wrote in 1950[30]

Political language—and with variations this is true of all political parties, from Conservatives to Anarchists—is designed to make lies sound truthful and murder respectable, and to give an appearance of solidity to pure wind.

The minister who openly admitted a lack of compliance with the international human rights code would be as worthy of a Bateman cartoon as would a minister who practised genuinely open government, or voluntarily gave Parliament a full and politically unattractive picture, warts and all. To acknowledge these obvious facts of political life is not cynical. Nor, on the other hand, is it naive to demand that our theoretically omnipotent and all-pervasive Parliament should be fully informed about these government games—whether of poker or of chess, and that Parliament should be allowed fair opportunities to participate as a significant player.

Parliament is not kept informed of other significant poker games played defensively abroad. One such game has been played for the past nine years in seeking to impede the movement to reform the outmoded, dilatory, and inefficient enforcement procedures of the European Convention. For years our Government opposed the creation of a single permanent European Court of Human Rights in place of the present two-tier Commission and Court. When they became isolated, they reluctantly agreed, last year, to work on a reforming Protocol to the Convention. Now, alone among the thirty-two European Governments involved in this process, they threaten to block the reform process because of the Home Office's objection to creating an automatic right of individual access to the Court, once domestic remedies have been exhausted. Parliament has not been informed of what is going on.

Parliament is kept in the dark about another poker game which is played at five-yearly intervals in New York between the Government's representatives and the UN Human Rights Committee. The Government then attempt to persuade the Human Rights Committee that the United Kingdom is fully complying with the obligations of Article 2 of the International Covenant to adopt such legislation or other measures as may be necessary to secure and give effect to the rights recognized in the Covenant, and to provide effective remedies for violations of those rights. In 1991, the Government incorporated those rights into the domestic law of Hong Kong.[31] Understandably, the Human Rights Committee remain sceptical about the failure to do the same in the United Kingdom itself.

---

[30] 'Politics and the English Language'. in the *Penguin Essays of George Orwell* (Penguin, 1984).
[31] By the Hong Kong Bill of Rights Ordinance 1991, and by amending the Letters Patent.

On the last occasion when this subject was before the Committee, in April 1985, Mr David Faulkner stated[32] optimistically that the Government hoped to submit new proposals on incorporating legislation at some future date. He went on to explain that:

The idea of a bill of rights enjoyed considerable support in some Parliamentary and legal circles, but was the subject of considerable opposition in other Parliamentary circles which argued that it was inappropriate to surrender some of the influence of the House of Commons to the judiciary and the legal profession . . . In view of the lack of broad agreement on such a proposal . . . the Government did not feel that it could impose its own position at the present time.

Several members of the Committee expressed their dissatisfaction with this position, and it will be interesting to see how they react to the next report, which is due this summer. There has, after all, been a sea change since 1985. The Lord Chief Justice, the Master of the Rolls, several Law Lords, and all of the Opposition parties have come out in favour of incorporation, joining Lord Scarman's twenty-year-old campaign.

Conclusion

For present purposes what matters is that the Government ought surely to submit their draft Report for debate in Parliament before submitting it to the Human Rights Committee. It is preposterous for the practice to continue of reporting on Parliamentary attitudes towards compliance with the Covenant without consulting Parliament.[33] By the same token, the Government should surely consult expert statutory bodies, such as the CRE and the EOCs, and should consult Parliament itself, before reporting to CERD, CEDAW, the ILO, the Human Rights Committee, and so on. All reports to and the responses from the Human Rights Committee and the specialized human rights bodies should surely be made widely available and should be published by HMSO.

The time has also come, I suggest, to establish Select Committees of the House of Lords, or of both Houses, to examine government legislative proposals, and government reporting to the international human rights bodies, and government policies, in the light of the United Kingdom's international human rights obligations. The House of Lords' Select Committee on the European Communities has recently reported[34] on scrutiny of the intergovernmental pillars of the European Union, emphasizing that this

[32] Human Rights Committee, 24th session, 53rd meeting, 11 April 1985, C.C.P.R./C./S.R. 593.

[33] See Hansard (HL), Vol. 553, 11 April 1994, W.A. 89.

[34] 28th Report, *House of Lords Scrutiny of the Inter-Governmental Pillars of the European Union*, 2 November 1993 (HL Paper 124).

subject should be supervised by national Parliaments, and that the key to effective and constructive supervision is to obtain documents in draft. The same is true of international human rights, if, in the Select Committee's words,[35] 'We intend to be vigilant in holding ministers to account in these areas'.

If we as citizens do indeed intend to be vigilant in holding ministers and their officials to account for exercising their powers in breach of our human rights, we need to compel them to take Parliament more seriously. To do that, we need to persuade Parliament itself to take human rights more seriously: by creating a Select Committee on Human Rights; by requiring relevant documents to be provided in draft; by drawing Parliament's attention to government proposals appearing to breach the international human rights codes; by incorporating Convention and Covenant rights and freedoms into domestic law; by being in the vanguard of strengthening the Convention's enforcement procedures, and by joining the seventy-four States which have already accepted the Optional Protocol to the Covenant (including most States Parties to the European Convention).

It is time to bring down the curtain on this comic opera, in which governments use Parliamentary sovereignty to shield themselves against effective accountability to Parliament and to the rule of law: both the international rule of law, and the rule of law of our own courts.

La Commedia e finita: the comedy is over.

---

[35] 28th Report, para. 65.

Appendix

Text of the European Convention as modified by Protocol 11
Convention for the Protection of Human Rights and Fundamental Freedoms

The governments signatory hereto, being members of the Council of Europe,

Considering the Universal Declaration of Human Rights proclaimed by the General Assembly of the United Nations on 10th December 1948;

Considering that this Declaration aims at securing the universal and effective recognition and observance of the Rights therein declared;

Considering that the aim of the Council of Europe is the achievement of greater unity between its members and that one of the methods by which that aim is to be pursued is the maintenance and further realisation of human rights and fundamental freedoms;

Reaffirming their profound belief in those fundamental freedoms which are the foundation of justice and peace in the world and are best maintained on the one hand by an effective political democracy and on the other by a common understanding and observance of the human rights upon which they depend;

Being resolved, as the governments of European countries which are like-minded and have a common heritage of political traditions, ideals, freedom and the rule of law, to take the first steps for the collective enforcement of certain of the rights stated in the Universal Declaration,

Have agreed as follows:

Article 1

Obligation to respect human rights

The High contracting Parties shall secure to everyone within their jurisdiction the rights and freedoms defined in Section I of this Convention.

SECTION I — RIGHTS AND FREEDOMS

Article 2

Right to life

1. Everyone's right to life shall be protected by law. No one shall be deprived of his life intentionally save in the execution of a sentence of a court following his conviction of a crime for which this penalty is provided by law.

2.   Deprivation of life shall not be regarded as inflicted in contravention of this Article when it results from the use of force which is no more than absolutely necessary:

  (a) in defence of any person from unlawful violence;
  (b) in order to effect a lawful arrest or to prevent the escape of a person lawfully detained;
  (c) in action lawfully taken for the purpose of quelling a riot or insurrection.

Article 3

Prohibition of torture

No one shall be subjected to torture or to inhuman or degrading treatment or punishment.

Article 4

Prohibition of slavery and forced labour

1.   No one shall be held in slavery or servitude.
2.   No one shall be required to perform forced or compulsory labour.
3.   For the purposes of this Article the term 'forced or compulsory labour' shall not include:

  (a) any work required to be done in the ordinary course of detention imposed according to the provisions of Article 5 of this Convention or during conditional release from such detention;
  (b) any service of a military character or, in the case of conscientious objectors in countries where they are recognised, service exacted instead of compulsory military service;
  (c) any service exacted in case of an emergency or calamity threatening the life or well-being of the community;
  (d) any work or service which forms part of normal civic obligations.

Article 5

Right to liberty and security

1.   Everyone has the right to liberty and security of the person. No one shall be deprived of his liberty save in the following cases and in accordance with a procedure prescribed by law:

  (a) the lawful detention of a person after conviction by a competent court;
  (b) the lawful arrest or detention of a person for non-compliance with the lawful order of a court or in order to secure the fulfilment of any obligation prescribed by law;
  (c) the lawful arrest or detention of a person effected for the purpose of bringing him before the competent legal authority on reasonable suspicion of having committed an offence or when it is reasonably considered necessary to prevent his committing an offence of fleeing after having done so;

(d) the detention of a minor by lawful order for the purpose of educational supervision or his lawful detention for the purpose of bringing him before the competent legal authority;

(e) the lawful detention of persons for the prevention of the spreading of infectious diseases, of persons of unsound mind, alcoholics or drug addicts or vagrants;

(f) the lawful arrest or detention of a person to prevent his effecting an unauthorised entry into the country or of a person against whom action is being taken with a view to deportation or extradition.

2. Everyone who is arrested shall be informed promptly, in a language which he understands, of the reasons for his arrest and of any charge against him.

3. Everyone arrested or detained in accordance with the provisions of paragraph (1)(c) of this Article shall be brought promptly before a judge or other officer authorised by law to exercise judicial power and shall be entitled to trial within a reasonable time or to release pending trial. Release may be conditioned by guarantees to appear for trial.

4. Everyone who is deprived of his liberty by arrest or detention shall be entitled to take proceedings by which the lawfulness of his detention shall be decided speedily by a court and his release ordered if the detention is not lawful.

5. Everyone who has been the victim of arrest or detention in contravention of the provisions of this Article shall have an enforceable right to compensation.

Article 6

Right to a fair trial

1. In the determination of his civil rights and obligations or of any criminal charge against him, everyone is entitled to a fair and public hearing within a reasonable time by an independent and impartial tribunal established by law. Judgment shall be pronounced publicly but the press and public may be excluded from all or part of the trial in the interests of morals, public order or national security in a democratic society, where the interests of juveniles or the protection of the private life of the parties so require, or to the extent strictly necessary in the opinion of the court in special circumstances where publicity would prejudice the interests of justice.

2. Everyone charged with a criminal offence shall be presumed innocent until proved guilty according to law.

3. Everyone charged with a criminal offence has the following minimum rights:

(a) to be informed promptly, in a language which he understands and in detail, of the nature and cause of the accusation against him;

(b) to have adequate time and facilities for the preparation of his defence;

(c) to defend himself in person or through legal assistance of his own choosing or, if he has not sufficient means to pay for legal assistance, to be given it free when the interests of justice so require;

(d) to examine or have examined witnesses against him and to obtain the attendance and examination of witnesses on his behalf under the same conditions as witnesses against him;

(e) to have the free assistance of an interpreter if he cannot understand or speak the language used in court.

Article 7

No punishment without law

1.   No one shall be held guilty of any criminal offence on account of any act or omission which did not constitute a criminal offence under national or international law at the time when it was committed. Nor shall a heavier penalty be imposed than the one that was applicable at the time the criminal offence was committed.

2.   This Article shall not prejudice the trial and punishment of any person for any act or omission which, at the time when it was committed, was criminal according to the general principles of law recognised by civilised nations.

Article 8

Right to respect for private and family life

1.   Everyone has the right to respect for his private and family life, his home and his correspondence.

2.   There shall be no interference by a public authority with the exercise of this right except such as is in accordance with the law and is necessary in a democratic society in the interests of national security, public safety or the economic well-being of the country, for the prevention of disorder or crime, for the protection of health or morals, or for the protection of the rights and freedoms of others.

Article 9

Freedom of thought, conscience and religion

1.   Everyone has the right to freedom of thought, conscience and religion; this right includes freedom to change his religion or belief and freedom, either alone or in community with others and in public or private, to manifest his religion or belief, in worship, teaching, practice and observance.

2.   Freedom to manifest one's religion or beliefs shall be subject only to such limitations as are prescribed by law and are necessary in a democratic society in the interests of public safety, for the protection of public order, health or morals, or for the protection of the rights and freedoms of others.

Article 10

Freedom of expression

1.   Everyone has the right to freedom of expression. This right shall include freedom to hold opinions and to receive and impart information and ideas without interference by public authority and regardless of frontiers. This Article shall not

prevent States from requiring the licensing of broadcasting, television or cinema enterprises.

2. The exercise of these freedoms, since it carries with it duties and responsibilities, may be subject to such formalities, conditions, restrictions or penalties as are prescribed by law and are necessary in a democratic society, in the interests of national security, territorial integrity or public safety, for the prevention of disorder or crime, for the protection of health or morals, for the protection of the reputation or rights of others, for preventing the disclosure of information received in confidence, or for maintaining the authority and impartiality of the judiciary.

Article 11

Freedom of assembly and association

1. Everyone has the right to freedom of peaceful assembly and to freedom of association with others, including the right to form and to join trade unions for the protection of his interests.

2. No restrictions shall be placed on the exercise of these rights other than such as are prescribed by law and are necessary in a democratic society in the interests of national security or public safety, for the protection of health or morals or for the protection of the rights and freedoms of others. This Article shall not prevent the imposition of lawful restrictions on the exercise of these rights by members of the armed forces, of the police or of the administration of the State.

Article 12

Right to marry

Men and women of marriageable age have the right to marry and to found a family, according to the national laws governing the exercise of this right.

Article 13

Right to an effective remedy

Everyone whose rights and freedoms as set forth in this Convention are violated shall have an effective remedy before a national authority notwithstanding that the violation has been committed by persons acting in an official capacity.

Article 14

Prohibition of discrimination

The enjoyment of the rights and freedoms set forth in this Convention shall be secured without discrimination on any ground such as sex, race, colour, language, religion, political or other opinion, national or social origin, association with a national minority, property, birth or other status.

Article 15

Derogation in time of emergency

1.   In time of war or other public emergency threatening the life of the nation any High Contracting Party may take measures derogating from its obligations under this Convention to the extent strictly required by the exigencies of the situation, provided that such measures are not inconsistent with its other obligations under international law.

2.   No derogation from Article 2, except in respect of deaths resulting from lawful acts of war, or from Articles 3, 4 (paragraph 1) and 7 shall be made under this provision.

3.   Any High Contracting Party availing itself of this right of derogation shall keep the Secretary General of the Council of Europe fully informed of the measures which it has taken and the reasons therefor. It shall also inform the Secretary General of the Council of Europe when such measures have ceased to operate and the provisions of the Convention are again being fully executed.

Article 16

Restrictions on political activity of aliens

Nothing in Articles 10, 11 and 14 shall be regarded as preventing the High Contracting Parties from imposing restrictions on the political activities of aliens.

Article 17

Prohibition of abuse of rights

Nothing in this Convention may be interpreted as implying for any State, group or person any right to engage in any activity or perform any act aimed at the destruction of any of the rights and freedoms set forth herein or at their limitation to a greater extent that is provided for in the Convention.

Article 18

Limitation on use of restrictions on rights

The restrictions permitted under this Convention to the said rights and freedoms shall not be applied for any purpose other than those for which they have been prescribed.

SECTION II — EUROPEAN COURT OF HUMAN RIGHTS

Article 19

Establishment of the Court

To ensure the observance of the engagements undertaken by the High Contracting Parties in the Convention and the protocols thereto, there shall be set up a

European Court of Human Rights, hereinafter referred to as 'the Court'. It shall function on a permanent basis.

Article 20

Number of judges

The Court shall consist of a number of judges equal to that of the High Contracting Parties.

Article 21

Criteria for office

1.   The judges shall be of high moral character and must either possess the qualifications required for appointment to high judicial office or be jurisconsults of recognised competence.

2.   The judges shall sit on the Court in their individual capacity.

3.   During their term of office the judges shall not engage in any activity which is incompatible with their independence, impartiality or with the demands of a full-time office; all questions arising from the application of this paragraph shall be decided by the Court.

Article 22

Election of judges

1.   The judges shall be elected by the Parliamentary Assembly with respect to each High Contracting Party by a majority of votes cast from a list of three candidates nominated by the High Contracting Party.

2.   The same procedure shall be followed to complete the Court in the event of the accession of new High Contracting Parties and in filling casual vacancies.

Article 23

Terms of office

1.   The judges shall be elected for a period of six years. They may be re-elected. However, the terms of office of one-half of the judges elected at the first election shall expire at the end of three years.

2.   The judges whose terms of office are to expire at the end of the initial period of three years shall be chosen by lot by the Secretary General of the Council of Europe immediately after their election.

3.   In order to ensure that, as far as possible, the terms of office of one-half of the judges are renewed every three years, the Parliamentary Assembly may decide, before proceeding to any subsequent election, that the term or terms of office of one

or more judges to be elected shall be for a period other than six years but not more than nine and not less than three years.

4. In cases where more than one term of office is involved and where the Parliamentary Assembly applies the preceding paragraph, the allocation of the terms of office shall be effected by a drawing of lots by the Secretary General of the Council of Europe immediately after the election.

5. A judge elected to replace a judge whose term of office has not expired shall hold office for the remainder of his predecessor's term.

6. The terms of office of judges shall expire when they reach the age of 70.

7. The judges shall hold office until replaced. They shall, however, continue to deal with such cases as they already have under consideration.

Article 24

Dismissal

No judge may be dismissed from his office unless the other judges decide by *a* majority of two-thirds that he has ceased to fulfil the required conditions.

Article 25

Registry and legal secretaries

The Court shall have a registry, the functions and organisation of which shall be laid down in the rules of the Court. The Court shall be assisted by legal secretaries.

Article 26

Plenary Court

The Plenary Court shall:
- (a) elect its President and one or two Vice-Presidents for a period of three years; they may be re-elected;
- (b) set up Chambers, constituted for a fixed period of time;
- (c) elect the Presidents of the Chambers of the Court; they may be re-elected;
- (d) adopt the rules of the Court; and
- (e) elect the Registrar and one or more Deputy Registrars.

Article 27

Committees, Chambers and Grand Chamber

1. To consider cases brought before it, the Court shall sit in committees of three judges, in Chambers of seven judges and in a Grand Chamber of seventeen judges. The Court's Chambers shall set up committees for a fixed period of time.

2. There shall sit as an *ex officio* member of the Chamber and the Grand Chamber the judge elected in respect of the State Party concerned or, if there is

none or if he is unable to sit, a person of its choice who shall sit in the capacity of judge.

3. The Grand Chamber shall also include the President of the Court, the Vice-Presidents, the Presidents of the Chambers and other judges chosen in accordance with the rules of the Court. When a case is referred to the Grand Chamber under Article 43, no judge from the Chamber which rendered the judgment shall sit in the Grand Chamber, with the exception of the President of the Chamber and the judge who sat in respect of the State Party concerned.

Article 28

Declaration of inadmissibility by committees

A committee may, by a unanimous vote, declare inadmissible or strike out of its list of cases an individual application submitted under Article 34 where such a decision can be taken without further examination. The decision shall be final.

Article 29

Decisions by Chambers on admissibility and merits

1. If no decision is taken under Article 28, a Chamber shall decide on the admissibility and merits of individual applications submitted under Article 34.

2. A Chamber shall decide on the admissibility and merits of inter-State applications submitted under Article 33.

3. The decision on admissibility shall be taken separately unless the Court, in exceptional cases, decides otherwise.

Article 30

Relinquishment of jurisdiction to the Grand Chamber

Where a case pending before a Chamber raises a serious question affecting the interpretation of the Convention or the protocols thereto or where the resolution of a question before it might have a result inconsistent with a judgment previously delivered by the Court, the Chamber may, at any time before it has rendered its judgment, relinquish jurisdiction in favour of the Grand Chamber, unless one of the parties to case objects.

Article 31

Powers of the Grand Chamber

The Grand Chamber shall
 (a) determine applications submitted either under Article 33 or Article 34 when a Chamber has relinquished jurisdiction under Article 30 or when the case has been referred to it under Article 43; and
 (b) consider requests for advisory opinions submitted under Article 47.

Appendix

Article 32

Jurisdiction of the Court

1. The jurisdiction of the Court shall extend to all matters concerning the interpretation and application of the Convention and the protocols thereto which are referred to it as provided in Articles 33, 34 and 47.

2. In the event of dispute as to whether the Court has jurisdiction, the Court shall decide.

Article 33

Inter-Stat cases

Any High Contracting Party may refer to the Court any alleged breach of the provisions of the Convention and the protocols thereto by another High Contracting Party.

Article 34

Individual applications

The Court may receive applications from any person, non-governmental organisation or group of individuals claiming to be the victim of a violation by one of the High Contracting Parties of the rights set forth in the Convention and the protocols thereto. The High Contracting Parties undertake not to hinder in any way the effective exercise of this right.

Article 35

Admissibility criteria

1. The Court may only deal with the matter after all domestic remedies have been exhausted, according to the generally recognised rules of international law, and within a period of six months from the date on which the final decision was taken.

2. The Court shall not deal with any individual application submitted under Article 34 that

    (a) is anonymous; or

    (b) is substantially the same as a matter that has already been examined by the Court or has already been submitted to another procedure of international investigation or settlement and contains no relevant new information.

3. The Court shall declare inadmissible any individual application submitted under Article 34 which it considers incompatible with the provisions of the Convention or the protocols thereto, manifestly ill-founded, or an abuse of the right of application.

4. The Court shall reject any application which it considers inadmissible under this Article. It may do so at any stage of the proceedings.

Article 36

Third-party intervention

1. In all cases before a Chamber or the Grand Chamber, a High Contracting Party one of whose nationals is an applicant shall have the right to submit written comments and to take part in the hearings.
2. The President of the Court may, in the interest of the proper administration of justice, invite any High Contracting Party which is not a party to the proceedings or any person concerned who is not the applicant to submit written comments or take part in the hearings.

Article 37

Striking out applications

1. The Court may at any stage of the proceedings decide to strike an application out of its list of cases where the circumstances lead to the conclusion that
   (a) the applicant does not intend to pursue his application; or
   (b) the matter has been resolved; or
   (c) for any other reason established by the Court, it is no longer justified to continue the examination of the application.
However, the Court shall continue the examination of the application if respect for human rights as defined in the Convention and the protocols thereto so requires.
2. The Court may decide to restore an application to its list of cases if it considers that the circumstances justify such a course.

Article 38

Examination of the case and friendly settlement proceedings

1. If the Court declares the application admissible, it shall
   (a) pursue the examination of the case, together with the representatives of the parties, and if need be, undertake an investigation, for the effective conduct of which the States concerned shall furnish all necessary facilities;
   (b) place itself at the disposal of the parties concerned with a view to securing a friendly settlement of the matter on the basis of respect for human rights as defined in the Convention and the protocols thereto.
2. Proceedings conducted under paragraph 1(b) shall be confidential.

Article 39

Finding of a friendly settlement

If a friendly settlement is effected, the Court shall strike the case out of its list by means of a decision which shall be confined to a brief statement of the facts and the solution reached.

Article 40

Public hearings and access to documents

1. Hearings shall be public unless the Court in exceptional circumstances decides otherwise.

2. Documents deposited with the Registrar shall be accessible to the public unless the President of the Court decides otherwise.

Article 41

Just satisfaction

If the Court finds that there has been a violation of the Convention or the protocols thereto, and if the internal law of the High Contracting Party concerned allows only partial reparation to be made, the Court shall, if necessary afford just satisfaction to the injured party.

Article 42

Judgments of Chambers

Judgments of Chambers shall become final in accordance with the provisions of Article 44, paragraph 2.

Article 43

Referral to the Grand Chamber

1. Within a period of three months from the date of the judgment of the Chamber, any party to the case may, in exceptional cases, request that the case be referred to the Grand Chamber.

2. A panel of five judges of the Grand Chamber shall accept the request if the case raises a serious question affecting the interpretation or application of the Convention or the protocols thereto, or a serious issue of general importance.

3. If the panel accepts the request, the Grand Chamber shall decide the case by means of a judgment.

Article 44

Final judgments

1. The judgment of the Grand Chamber shall be final.
2. The judgment of a Chamber shall become final
    (a) when the parties declare that they will not request that the case be referred to the Grand Chamber; or

(b) three months after the date of the judgment, if reference of the case to the Grand Chamber has not been requested; or

(c) when the panel of the Grand Chamber rejects the request to refer under Article 43.

3. The final judgment shall be published.

Article 45

Reasons for judgments and decisions

1. Reasons shall be given for judgments as well as for decisions declaring applications admissible or inadmissible.

2. If a judgment does not represent, in whole or in part, the unanimous opinion of the judges, any judge shall be entitled to deliver a separate opinion.

Article 46

Binding force and execution of judgments

1. The High Contracting Parties undertake to abide by the final judgment of the Court in any case where they are parties.

2. The final judgment of the Court shall be transmitted to the Committee of Ministers, which shall supervise its execution.

Article 47

Advisory opinions

1. The Court may, at the request of the Committee of Ministers, give advisory opinions on legal questions concerning the interpretation of the Convention and the protocols thereto.

2. Such opinions shall not deal with any question relating to the content or scope of the rights or freedoms defined in Section I of the Convention and the protocols thereto, or with any other question which the Court or the Committee of Ministers might have to consider in consequence of any such proceedings as could be instituted in accordance with the Convention.

3. Decisions of the Committee of Ministers to request an advisory opinion of the Court shall require a majority vote of the representatives entitled to sit on the Committee.

Article 48

Advisory Jurisdiction of the Court

The Court shall decide whether a request for an advisory opinion submitted by the Committee of Ministers is within its competence as defined in Article 47.

Article 49

Reasons for advisory opinions

1.   Reasons shall be given for advisory opinions of the Court.

2.   If the advisory opinion does not represent, in whole or in part, the unanimous opinion of the judges, any judge shall be entitled to deliver a separate opinion.

3.   Advisory opinions of the Court shall be communicated to the Committee of Ministers.

Article 50

Expenditure on the Court

The expenditure on the Court shall be borne by the Council of Europe.

Article 51

Privileges and immunities of judges

The judges shall be entitled, during the exercise of their functions, to the privileges and immunities provided for in Article 40 of the Statute of the Council of Europe and in the agreements made thereunder.

SECTION III — MISCELLANEOUS PROVISIONS

Article 52

Enquiries by the Secretary General

On receipt of a request from the Secretary General of the Council of Europe any High Contracting Party shall furnish an explanation of the manner in which its internal law ensures the effective implementation of any of the provisions of the Convention.

Article 53

Safeguard for existing human rights

Nothing in this Convention shall be construed as limiting or derogating from any of the human rights and fundamental freedoms which may be ensured under the laws of any High Contracting Party or under any other agreement to which it is a Party.

Article 54

Powers of the Committee of Ministers

Nothing in this Convention shall prejudice the powers conferred on the Committee of Ministers by the Statute of the Council of Europe.

Article 55

Exclusion of other means of dispute settlement

The High Contracting Parties agree that, except by special agreement, they will not avail themselves of treaties, conventions or declarations in force between them for the purpose of submitting, by way of petition, a dispute arising out of the interpretation or application of this Convention to a means of settlement other than those provided for in this Convention.

Article 56

Territorial application

1. Any State may at the time of its ratification or at any time thereafter declare by notification addressed to the Secretary General of the Council of Europe that the present Convention shall, subject to paragraph 4 of this Article, extend to all or any of the territories for whose international relations it is responsible.

2. The Convention shall extend to the territory or territories named in the notification as from the thirtieth day after the receipt of this notification by the Secretary General of the Council of Europe.

3. The provisions of this Convention shall be applied in such territories with due regard, however, to local requirements.

4. Any State which has made a declaration in accordance with paragraph 1 of this Article may at any time thereafter declare on behalf of one or more of the territories to which the declaration relates that it accepts the competence of the Court to receive applications from individuals, non-governmental organisations or groups of individuals as provided in Article 34 of the Convention.

Article 57

Reservations

1. Any State may, when signing this Convention or when depositing its instrument of ratification, make a reservation in respect of any particular provision of the Convention to the extent that any law then in force in its territory is not in conformity with the provision. Reservations of a general character shall not be permitted under this Article.

2. Any reservation made under this Article shall contain a brief statement of the law concerned.

Article 58

Denunciation

1. A High Contracting Party may denounce the present Convention only after the expiry of five years from the date on which it became a party to it and after six months' notice contained in a notification addressed to the Secretary General of the Council of Europe, who shall inform the other High Contracting Parties.

2.   Such a denunciation shall not have the effect of releasing the High Contracting Party concerned from its obligations under this Convention in respect of any act which, being capable of constituting a violation of such obligations, may have been performed by it before the date at which the denunciation became effective.

3.   Any High Contracting Party which shall cease to be a member of the Council of Europe shall cease to be a Party to this Convention under the same conditions.

4.   The Convention may be denounced in accordance with the provisions of the preceding paragraphs in respect of any territory to which it has been declared to extend under the terms of Article 56.

Article 59

Signature and ratification

1.   This Convention shall be open to the signature of the members of the Council of Europe. It shall be ratified. Ratifications shall be deposited with the Secretary General of the Council of Europe.

2.   The present Convention shall come into force after the deposit of ten instruments of ratification.

3.   As regards any signatory ratifying subsequently, the Convention shall come into force at the date of the deposit of its instrument of ratification.

4.   The Secretary General of the Council of Europe shall notify all the members of the Council of Europe of the entry into force of the Convention, the names of the High Contracting Parties who have ratified it, and the deposit of all instruments of ratification which may be effected subsequently.

Done at Rome this 4th day of November 1950, in English and French, both texts being equally authentic, in a single copy which shall remain deposited in the archives of the Council of Europe. The Secretary General shall transmit certified copies to each of the signatories.

Protocol No. 1

The governments signatory hereto, being members of the Council of Europe

Being resolved to take steps to ensure the collective enforcement of certain rights and freedoms other than those already included in Section I of the Convention for the Protection of Human Rights and Fundamental Freedoms signed at Rome on 4 November 1950 (hereinafter referred to as 'the Convention'),

Have agreed as follows:

Article 1

Protection of property

Every natural or legal person is entitled to the peaceful enjoyment of his possessions. No one shall be deprived of his possessions except in the public interest and subject to the conditions provided for by law and by the general principles of international law.

The preceding provisions shall not, however, in any way impair the right of a State to enforce such laws as it deems necessary to control the use of property in accordance with the general interest or to secure the payment of taxes or other contributions or penalties.

Article 2

Right to education

No person shall be denied the right to education. In the exercise of any functions which it assumes in relation to education and to teaching, the State shall respect the right of parents to ensure such education and teaching in conformity with their own religious and philosophical convictions.

Article 3

Right to free elections

The High Contracting Parties undertake to hold free elections at reasonable intervals by secret ballot, under conditions which will ensure the free expression of the opinion of the people in the choice of the legislature.

Article 4

Territorial application

Any High Contracting Party may at the time of signature or ratification or at any time thereafter communicate to the Secretary General of the Council of Europe a declaration stating the extent to which it undertakes that the provisions of the present Protocol shall apply to such of the territories for the international relations of which it is responsible as are named therein.

Any High Contracting Party which has communicated a declaration in virtue of the preceding paragraph may from time to time communicate a further declaration modifying the terms of any former declaration or terminating the application of the provisions of this Protocol in respect of any territory.

A declaration made in accordance with this Article shall be deemed to have been made in accordance with paragraph 1 of Article 56 of the Convention.

Article 5

Relationship to the Convention

As between the High Contracting Parties the provisions of Articles 1, 2, 3 and 4 of this Protocol shall be regarded as additional articles to the Convention and all the provisions of the Convention shall apply accordingly.

Article 6

Signature and ratification

This Protocol shall be open for signature by the members of the Council of Europe, who are the signatories of the Convention; it shall be ratified at the same time as or after the ratification of the Convention. It shall enter into force after the deposit of ten instruments of ratification. As regards any signatory ratifying subsequently, the Protocol shall enter into force at the date of the deposit of its instrument of ratification.

The instruments of ratification shall be deposited with the Secretary General of the Council of Europe, who will notify all members of the names of those who have ratified.

Done at Paris on the 20th day of March 1952, in English and French, both texts being equally authentic, in a single copy which shall remain deposited in the archives of the Council of Europe. The Secretary General shall transmit a certified copy to each of the signatory governments.

[Protocol No. 2 becomes otiose, since the provisions on the Court's competence to give advisory opinions is incorporated in Articles 47 to 49 of the Convention.]

[Protocol No. 3 has become otiose; it modified the procedure of the Commission by abolishing the system of sub-commissions.]

Protocol No. 4 to the Convention for the Protection of Human Rights and Fundamental Freedoms securing certain Rights and Freedoms other than those already included in the Convention and in the First Protocol thereto

The governments signatory hereto, being members of the Council of Europe

Being resolved to take steps to ensure the collective enforcement of certain rights and freedoms other than those already included in Section I of the Convention for the Protection of Human Rights and Fundamental Freedoms signed at Rome on 4 November 1950 (hereinafter referred to as 'the Convention') and in Articles 1 to 3 of the First Protocol to the Convention, signed at Paris on 20 March 1952

Have agreed as follows:

Article 1

Prohibition of imprisonment for debt

No one shall be deprived of his liberty merely on the ground of inability to fulfil a contractual obligation.

Article 2

Freedom of movement

1. Everyone lawfully within the territory of a State shall, within that territory, have the right to liberty of movement and freedom to choose his residence.

2.   Everyone shall be free to leave any country, including his own.

3.   No restrictions shall be placed on the exercise of these rights other than such as are in accordance with law and are necessary in a democratic society in the interests of national security or public safety, for the maintenance of the *order public*, for the prevention of crime, for the protection of health or morals or for the protection of the rights and freedoms of others.

4.   The rights set forth in paragraph 1 may also be subject in particular areas, to restrictions imposed in accordance with law and justified by the public interest in a democratic society.

Article 3

Prohibition of expulsion of nationals

1.   No one shall be expelled, by means either of an individual or of a collective measure, from the territory of the State of which he is a national.

2.   No one shall be deprived of the right to enter the territory of the State of which he is a national.

Article 4

Prohibition of collective expulsion of aliens

Collective expulsion of aliens is prohibited.

Article 5

Territorial application

1.   Any High Contracting Party may, at the time of signature or ratification of this protocol, or at any time thereafter, communicate to the Secretary General of the Council of Europe a declaration stating the extent to which it undertakes that the provisions of this Protocol shall apply to such of the territories for the international relations of which it is responsible as are named therein.

2.   Any High Contracting Party which has communicated a declaration in virtue of the preceding paragraph may, from time to time, communicate a further declaration modifying the terms of any former declaration or terminating the application of the provisions of this Protocol in respect of any territory.

3.   A declaration made in accordance with this Article shall be deemed to have been made in accordance with paragraph 1 of Article 56 of the Convention.

4.   The territory of any State to which this Protocol applies by virtue of ratification or acceptance by that State, and each territory to which this Protocol is applied by virtue of a declaration by that State under this Article, shall be treated as separate territories for the purpose of the references in Articles 2 and 3 to the territory of a State.

5.   Any State which has made a declaration in accordance with paragraph 1 or 2 of this Article may at any time thereafter declare on behalf of one or more of the

territories to which the declaration relates that it accepts the competence of the Court to receive applications from individuals, non-governmental organizations or groups of individuals as provided in Article 34 of the Convention in respect of all or any of Articles 1 to 4 of this Protocol.

Article 6

Relationship to the Convention

As between the High Contracting Parties the provisions of Articles 1 to 5 of this Protocol shall be regarded as additional Articles to the Convention, and the provisions of the Convention shall apply accordingly.

Article 7

Signature and ratification

1.   This Protocol shall be open for signature by the members of the Council of Europe who are signatories of the Convention; it shall be ratified at the same time as or after the ratification of the Convention. It shall enter into force after the deposit of five instruments of ratification. As regards any signatory ratifying subsequently, the Protocol shall enter into force at the date of the deposit of its instrument of ratification.

2.   The instruments of ratification shall be deposited with the Secretary General of the Council of Europe, who will notify all members of the names of those who have ratified.

In witness whereof the undersigned, being duly authorised thereto, have signed this Protocol.

Done at Strasbourg, this 16th day of September 1963, in English and in French, both texts being equally authoritative, in a single copy which shall remain deposited in the archives of the Council of Europe. The Secretary General shall transmit certified copies to each of the signatories.

[Protocol No. 5 has become otiose; it concerned the procedure for the election of members of the Commission and Court.]

Protocol No. 6 to the Convention for the Protection of Human Rights and Fundamental Freedoms concerning the abolition of the death penalty

The member States of the Council of Europe, signatory to this Protocol to the Convention for the Protection of Human Rights and Fundamental Freedoms, signed at Rome on 4 November 1950 (hereinafter referred to as 'the Convention'),

Considering that the evolution that has occurred in several member States of the Council of Europe expresses a general tendency in favour of the abolition of the death penalty;

Have agreed as follows:

Article 1

Abolition of the death penalty

The death penalty shall be abolished. No one shall be condemned to such penalty or executed.

Article 2

Death penalty in time of war

A State may make provision in its law for the death penalty in respect of acts committed in time of war or of imminent threat of war; such penalty shall be applied only in the instances laid down in the law and in accordance with its provisions. The State shall communicate to the Secretary General of the Council of Europe the relevant provisions of that law.

Article 3

Prohibition of derogations

No derogation from the provisions of this Protocol shall be made under Article 15 of the Convention.

Article 4

Prohibition of reservations

No reservation may be made under Article 57 of the Convention in respect of the provisions of this Protocol.

Article 5

Territorial application

1.   Any State may at the time of signature or when depositing its instrument of ratification, acceptance or approval, specify the territory or territories to which this Protocol shall apply.

2.   Any State may at any later date, by a declaration addressed to the Secretary General of the Council of Europe, extend the application of this Protocol to any other territory specified in the declaration. In respect of such territory the Protocol shall enter into force on the first day of the month following the date of receipt of such declaration by the Secretary General.

3.   Any declaration made under the two preceding paragraphs may, in respect of any territory specified in such declaration, be withdrawn by a notification addressed to the Secretary General. The withdrawal shall become effective on the first day of the month following the date of receipt of such notification by the Secretary General.

Article 6

Relationship to the Convention

As between the States Parties the provisions of Articles 1 to 5 of this Protocol shall be regarded as additional articles to the convention and all the provisions of the Convention shall apply accordingly.

Article 7

Signature and ratification

The Protocol shall be open for signature by the member States of the Council of Europe, signatories to the Convention. It shall be subject to ratification, acceptance or approval. A member State of the Council of Europe may not ratify, accept or approve this Protocol unless it has, simultaneously or previously, ratified the Convention. Instruments of ratification, acceptance or approval shall be deposited with the Secretary General of the Council of Europe.

Article 8

Entry into force

1. This Protocol shall enter into force on the first day of the month following the date on which five member States of the Council of Europe have expressed their consent to be bound by the Protocol in accordance with the provisions of Article 7.

2. In respect of any member State which subsequently expresses its consent to be bound by it, the Protocol shall enter into force on the first day of the month following the date of the deposit of the instrument of ratification, acceptance or approval.

Article 9

Depositary functions

The Secretary General of the Council of Europe shall notify the member States of the Council of:
   (a) any signature;
   (b) the deposit of any instrument of ratification, acceptance or approval;
   (c) any date of entry into force of this Protocol in accordance with Articles 5 and 8;
   (d) any other act, notification or communication relating to this Protocol.
In witness whereof the undersigned, being duly authorised thereto, have signed this Protocol.

Done at Strasbourg, this 28th day of April 1983, in English and in French, both texts being equally authentic, in a single copy which shall be deposited in the archives of the Council of Europe. The Secretary General of the Council of Europe shall transmit certified copies to each member State of the Council of Europe.

Protocol No. 7 to the Convention for the Protection of Human Rights and Fundamental Freedoms

The member States of the Council of Europe signatory hereto,

Being resolved to ensure the collective enforcement of certain rights and freedoms by means of the Convention for the Protection of Human Rights and Fundamental Freedoms signed at Rome on 4 November 1950 (hereinafter referred to as 'the Convention'),

Have agreed as follows:

Article 1

Procedural safeguards relating to expulsion of aliens

1. An alien lawfully resident in the territory of a State shall not be expelled therefrom except in pursuance of a decision reached in accordance with law and shall be allowed:
   (a) to submit reasons against his expulsion;
   (b) to have his case reviewed; and
   (c) to be represented for these purposes before the competent authority or a person or persons designated by that authority.

2. An alien may be expelled before the exercise of his rights under paragraph 1 (a), (b) and (c) of this Article, when such expulsion is necessary in the interests of public order or is grounded on reasons of national security.

Article 2

Right of appeal in criminal matters

1. Everyone convicted of a criminal offence by a tribunal shall have the right to have his conviction or sentence reviewed by a higher tribunal. The exercise of this right, including the grounds on which it may be exercised, shall be governed by law.

2. This right may be subject to exceptions in regard to offences of a minor character, as prescribed by law, or in cases in which the person concerned was tried in the first instance by the highest tribunal or was convicted following an appeal against acquittal.

Article 3

Compensation for wrongful conviction

When a person has by a final decision been convicted of a criminal offence and when subsequently his conviction has been reversed, or he has been pardoned, on the ground that a new or newly discovered fact shows conclusively that there has been a miscarriage of justice, the person who has suffered punishment as a result of such conviction shall be compensated according to the law or the practice of the

State concerned, unless it is proved that the non-disclosure of the unknown fact in time is wholly or partly attributable to him.

Article 4

Right not to be tried or punished twice

1. No one shall be liable to be tried or punished again in criminal proceedings under the jurisdiction of the same State for an offence for which he has already been finally acquitted or convicted in accordance with the law and penal procedure of that State.

2. The provisions of the preceding paragraph shall not prevent the reopening of the case in accordance with the law and penal procedure of the State concerned, if there is evidence of new or newly discovered facts, or if there has been a fundamental defect in the previous proceedings, which could affect the outcome of the case.

3. No derogation from this Article shall be made under Article 15 of the Convention.

Article 5

Equality between spouses

Spouses shall enjoy equality of rights and relationships of a private law character between them, and in their relations with their children, as to marriage, during marriage and in the event of its dissolution. This Article shall not prevent States from taking such measures as are necessary in the interests of the children.

Article 6

Territorial application

1. Any State may at the time of signature or when depositing its instrument of ratification, acceptance or approval, specify the territory or territories to which the Protocol shall apply and state the extent to which it undertakes that the provisions of this Protocol shall apply to such territory or territories.

2. Any State may at any later date, by a declaration addressed to the Secretary General of the Council of Europe, extend the application of this Protocol to any other territory specified in the declaration. In respect of such territory the Protocol shall enter into force on the first day of the month following the expiration of a period of two months after the date of receipt of such notification by the Secretary General.

3. Any declaration made under the preceding two paragraphs may, in respect of any territory specified in such declaration, be withdrawn or modified by a notification addressed to the Secretary General. The withdrawal or modification shall become effective on the first day of the month following the expiration of a period of two months after the date of receipt of such notification by the Secretary General.

4.   A declaration made in accordance with this Article shall be deemed to have been made in accordance with paragraph 1 of Article 56 of the Convention.

5.   The territory of any State to which this Protocol applies by virtue of ratification, acceptance or approval by that State, and each territory to which this Protocol is applied by virtue of a declaration by that State under this Article, may be treated as separate territories for the purpose of the reference in Article 1 to the territory of a State.

6.   Any State which has made a declaration in accordance with paragraph 1 or 2 of this Article may at any time thereafter declare on behalf of one or more of the territories to which the declaration relates that it accepts the competence of the Court to receive applications from individuals, non-governmental organisations or groups of individuals as provided in Article 34 of the Convention in respect of Articles 1 to 5 of this Protocol.

Article 7

Relationship to the Convention

As between the States Parties, the provisions of Articles 1 to 6 of this protocol shall be regarded as additional Articles to the Convention, and all the provisions of the Convention shall apply accordingly.

Article 8

Signature and ratification

This Protocol shall be open for signature by member States of the Council of Europe which have signed the Convention. It is subject to ratification, acceptance or approval. A member State of the Council of Europe may not ratify, accept or approve this Protocol without previously or simultaneously ratifying the Convention. Instruments of ratification, acceptance or approval shall be deposited with the Secretary General of the Council of Europe.

Article 9

Entry into force

1.   This Protocol shall enter into force on the first day of the month following the expiration of a period of two months after the date on which seven member States of the Council of Europe have expressed their consent to be bound by the Protocol in accordance with the provisions of Article 8.

2.   In respect of any member State which subsequently expresses its consent to be bound by it, the Protocol shall enter into force on the first day of the month following the expiration of a period of two months after the date of the deposit of the instrument of ratification, acceptance or approval.

Article 10

Depositary functions

The Secretary General of the Council of Europe shall notify all the member States of the Council of Europe of:

(a) any signature;

(b) the deposit of any instrument of ratification, acceptance or approval;

(c) any date of entry into force of this protocol in accordance with Articles 6 and 9;

(d) any other act, notification or declaration relating to this Protocol.

In witness whereof the undersigned, being duly authorised thereto, have signed this Protocol.

Done at Strasbourg, this 22nd day of November 1984, in English and French, both texts being equally authentic, in a single copy which shall be deposited in the archives of the Council of Europe. The Secretary General of the Council of Europe shall transmit certified copies to each member State of the Council of Europe.

[Protocol No. 8 has become otiose; it amended certain provisions relating to the Commission and the Court.]

[Protocol No. 9 has become otiose; it amended certain provisions of the Convention to improve the position of individual applicants.]

[Protocol No. 10 has become otiose; it changed the majority required for a decision of the Committee of Ministers under the original Article 32.]

Protocol No. 11 to the Convention for the Protection of Human Rights and Fundamental Freedoms, restructuring the control machinery established thereby

The member States of the Council of Europe, signatories to this Protocol to the Convention for the Protection of Human Rights and Fundamental Freedoms, signed at Rome on 4 November 1950 (hereinafter referred to as 'the Convention'),

Considering the urgent need to restructure the control machinery established by the Convention in order to maintain and improve the efficiency of its protection of human rights and fundamental freedoms, mainly in view of the increase in the number of applications and the growing membership of the Council of Europe;

Considering that it is therefore desirable to amend certain provisions of the Convention with a view, in particular, to replacing the existing European Commission and Court of Human Rights with a new permanent Court;

Having regard to Resolution No. 1 adopted at the European Ministerial Conference on Human Rights, held in Vienna on 19 and 20 March 1985;

Having regard to recommendation 1194 (1992), adopted by the Parliamentary Assembly of the Council of Europe on 6 October 1992;

Having regard to the decision taken on reform of the Convention control machinery by the Heads of State and Government of the Council of Europe member States in the Vienna Declaration on 9 October 1993,

Have agreed as follows:

Article 1

[Replaces the text of Sections II to IV of the Convention and of Protocol No. 2; the amendments have been incorporated in the text set out above.]

Article 2

[Amends the text of other provisions of the Convention and Protocols; the amendments have been incorporated in the text set out above.]

Article 3

1.   This Protocol shall be open for signature by member States of the Council of Europe signatories to the Convention, which may express their consent to be bound by
   (a) signature without reservation as to ratification, acceptance or approval; or
   (b) signature subject to ratification, acceptance or approval, followed by ratification, acceptance or approval.
2.   The instruments of ratification, acceptance or approval shall be deposited with the Secretary General of the Council of Europe.

Article 4

This Protocol shall enter into force on the first day of the month following the expiration of a period of one year after the date on which all Parties to the Convention have expressed their consent to be bound by the Protocol in accordance with the provisions of Article 3. The election of new judges may take place, and any further necessary steps may be taken to establish the new Court, in accordance with the provisions of this Protocol from the date on which all Parties to the Convention have expressed their consent to be bound by the Protocol.

Article 5

1.   Without prejudice to the provisions in paragraphs 3 and 4 below, the terms of office of the judges, members of the Commission, Registrar and Deputy registrar shall expire at the date of entry into force of this Protocol.
2.   Applications pending before the Commission which have not been declared admissible at the date of the entry into force of this Protocol shall be examined by the Court in accordance with the provisions of this Protocol.
3.   Applications which have been declared admissible at the date of the entry into force of this Protocol shall continue to be dealt with by members of the Commission within a period of one year thereafter. Any applications the examination of which has not been completed within the aforesaid period shall be transmitted to the Court which shall examine them as admissible cases in accordance with the provisions of this Protocol.

4. With respect to applications in which the Commission, after the entry into force of this Protocol, has adopted a report in accordance with former Article 31 of the Convention, the report shall be transmitted to the parties, who shall not be at liberty to publish it. In accordance with the provisions applicable prior to the entry into force of this Protocol, a case may be referred to the Court. The panel of the Grand Chamber shall determine whether one of the Chambers or the Grand Chamber shall decide the case. If the case is decided by a Chamber, the decision of the Chamber shall be final. Cases not referred to the Court shall be dealt with by the Committee of Ministers acting in accordance with the provisions of former Article 32 of the Convention.

5. Cases pending before the Court which have not been decided at the date of entry into force of this Protocol shall be transmitted to the Grand Chamber of the Court, which shall examine them in accordance with the provisions of this Protocol.

6. Cases pending before the Committee of Ministers which have not been decided under former Article 32 of the Convention at the date of entry into force of this Protocol shall be completed by the Committee of Ministers acting in accordance with that Article.

Article 6

Where a High Contracting Party had made a declaration recognising the competence of the Commission or the jurisdiction of the Court under former Article 25 or 46 of the Convention with respect to matters arising after or based on facts occurring subsequent to any such declaration, this limitation shall remain valid for the jurisdiction of the Court under this Protocol.

Article 7

The Secretary General of the Council of Europe shall notify the member States of the Council of:

(a) any signature;

(b) the deposit of any instrument of ratification, acceptance or approval;

(c) the date of entry into force of this Protocol or of any of its provisions in accordance with Article 4; and

(d) any other act, notification or communication relating to this Protocol.

In witness whereof the undersigned, being duly authorised thereto, have signed this Protocol.

Done at Strasbourg, this 11th day of May 1994 in English and French, both texts being equally authentic, in a single copy which shall be deposited in the archives of the Council of Europe. The Secretary General of the Council of Europe shall transmit certified copies to each member State of the Council of Europe.

AOI - 9918

KD
4080
Z9
H86
1996

5/27/97
APP